W9-CFV-308

Better Golf

Better Golf

A Skill Building Approach

Julius Richardson

with

Mark Gearen

Warde Publishers

Palo Alto, California

Warde Publishers, Inc.
530 University Avenue, Suite 102-7
Palo Alto, CA 94301
(800) 699-2733

Publisher's Cataloging-In-Publication Data
(Prepared by The Donohue Group, Inc.)
Richardson, Julius.
    Better golf : a skill building approach / Julius Richardson and Mark Gearen.
       p.   : ill.   ; cm.
       Includes index.
    ISBN: 1-886346-53-4
1. Golf--Handbooks, manuals, etc.   2. Swing (Golf)--Handbooks, manuals, etc.   I. Gearen, Mark. II. Title.
GV979.S525   R53 2005
796.352

Printed in the United States of America
10 9 8 7 6 5 4 3 2 1   08   07   06   05

Warde Publishers, Inc. and the authors disclaim responsibility for adverse effects or consequences from the misapplication or injudicious use of the information contained in this book. Mention of resources and associations does not imply endorsement by Warde Publishers, Inc. or the authors.

Illustrations: Phil Franke
Photo model: Michael Freeman

Photo credits: Page 2, Jeff Agard; page 3, Ed Falk and Carole Parker; pages 10–11, ship-in-bottle concept provided by Artem Popov; model provided by Donald Hubbard; page 18, Bowling sequence: from J. Jowdy, *Bowling Execution,* pages 102 and 103. Copyright by John Jowdy. Reprinted by permission from Human Kinetics (Champaign, IL).

Design: Detta Penna; Copyeditor: Pat Brewer;
Composition and paging: Penna Design and Production.

I dedicate this book to the angels in heaven, may they continue to look down on this humble, determined, persistent soul.

And to my wife, Margaret, and my six children:
Rose Marie, Julius Jr., Julieanne, Sabrina, Gail, and Kimberly.

And to my students who I encourage to practice, practice, practice, and I clearly state to them "Please don't embarrass me."

—Julius Richardson

To the memories of Jack and Virginia Gearen,
and Mary Gearen Barbato.

—Mark Gearen

Contents

Foreword
by Bob Toski

I was delighted to be asked to write a foreward for Julius Richardson's book, because I think Julius is a breath of fresh air in the world of golf instruction. He gives golfers something they can really use.

Julius is very successful as a teacher, and I think it's because he has a much better understanding of how the average player learns. He helps students prepare, so they can have more fun on the golf course.

Julius' teaching is based on building control, starting with the short shots and going forward from there. That's also how I teach. I tell my students, "little success patterns create big success patterns."

You save your students a lot of strokes when you begin them with short shots. The student gets to a lower handicap much faster that way. When you learn to play from the green to the tee, you'll learn to get from the tee to the green quicker.

I also like how Julius' teaching relates to players at all levels. When I got off the tour after being the leading money winner in 1954 and began teaching, everybody wanted to take lessons from me. But in retrospect, my first five years of teaching were not very good, because I taught all players as if they were strong, athletic, and could shoot in the seventies! You only mature as a teacher when you learn to teach the high handicap players, players who don't get to practice, who don't have a lot of power, who have flexibility issues, —players who have difficulty with the game. You eventually find that your greatest satisfaction as a teacher is in helping people who find golf difficult. For players who are struggling, or frustrated, Julius provides great building blocks to get better.

I like Julius' technique of hands-on drills, what he calls "bench drills." These are like physical therapy, in a sense, and they're especially effective for players who have trouble getting the feel of the body motion in the swing.

Julius also uses what I call "phantom teaching"—teaching without a club and ball. Phantom teaching is extremely effective because players react differently when there's no ball there. They're not trying to overpower the swing, or overpower this object at the base of their feet. They relax more, they're more aware of their feelings, what their bodies are doing, and they learn much better.

Julius has a very good eye, a trained eye. He knows about head position, body position, and alignment, and he's broken it down into body parts. When he combines that breakdown with phantom teaching, he's able to get players into good habits, and break bad habits very quickly.

I think many pros could learn from Julius, because so many of them don't seem to know how to prepare their players. They depend on video a good deal—Julius doesn't use video and neither do I. Video can only do so much—what you really need is to get people into good habits, and I don't think that happens watching a video screen. Julius' method is to get you to understand how to control your golf swing so that you can prepare for success instead of disaster.

Not everyone is going to agree with Julius, because no one has ever developed this preparation to the degree that he has. But I agree with Julius—he's trying to tell the world that the average pro doesn't prepare his pupils as fully as he should—and he's right. With a little training of this kind, players can shoot lower scores and have a lot more fun playing the game.

Acknowledgments

"When you can do the common things of life in an uncommon way, you will command the attention of the world."
—George Washington Carver, scientist, teacher, and inventor

Many experiences formed the basis of my teaching style, and many people influenced my ultimate teaching method. This is my opportunity to thank some of them.

Percy Boomer's book, *On Learning Golf,* started me on my journey to understanding the mechanics of the swing. Richard Grout's instruction put me on a path to becoming a scratch golfer and started the evolution of my teaching style.

The biggest influence on my teaching approach was my military service experience. The Army took people from all walks of life and trained them to successfully perform complex tasks where the risk of failure was extreme. My golf instruction approach involves dividing the complex into simple digestible concepts—on providing basic building blocks upon which to *build* a golf swing. Would you teach a soldier to shoot a rifle by handing him bullets without a firm understanding of basic safety and marksmanship concepts?

Many students, friends, and relatives encouraged me to write this book—I have room to mention only a few of them. My parents, John and Marie Richardson, set the stage for all the good things that happened in my life. My mother was an angel, and my father was a benevolent dictator and the kindest enforcer of life's rules you'd ever want to meet. My lovely wife, Margaret, has accepted my passion, enthusiasm, and addiction to golf for the past 52 years. She has supported me when I was out of town for long periods and when I was at home but my mind was on golf. The support of my daughters, Julieanna, Sabrina, Gail, and Kimberly, helped me finish this book.

Thanks to the various golf professionals and golf club managers who allowed me to ply my craft. To Joe Ferncez, Director of Golf at Naval Station Great Lakes, who opened the door for my professional career by providing me the opportunity—*at age 65*—to teach at a golf course. To Dan Kraft, who replaced Joe as Director of Golf and made me feel like a part of his staff. To Lou Harris, the Director of Golf at MacDill Air Force Base in Tampa, Florida, who allowed me to continue my teaching career and provided outstanding support during my tenure at MacDill. To Troy Gann, Director of Golf at Randolph Oaks Golf Course at Randolph Air Force Base in San Antonio, Texas. To Frank Jemsek, whose family owns and operates three of the finest public golf facilities in the Chicago area, who invited me to teach at Pine Meadows Golf Club. To my good friend Bob Toski, a twenty-time PGA tour winner, World Golf Teachers Hall of Fame inductee, and one of *Golf Magazine's Top 100 Teaching Professionals in America,* who wrote the Foreword to this book. To Wally Armstrong, nationally acclaimed golf instructor and writer, who found the time to help me find my publisher despite his busy schedule.

The United States Golf Teachers Federation (USGTF) also greatly contributed to my success as an instructor. Geoff Bryant, USGTF President, gave me the opportunity to teach at the USGTF facility at Port St. Lucie, Florida. Members of his outstanding staff: Thomas Wartelle, Stephanie Morris, Bob Wyatt, and Advisory Board Member Michael Levine all provided support and encouragement. Ben Jackson, former Vice President and Managing Editor of the USGTF magazine, and now Golf Professional at the New England Golf Academy at the Stonington Country Club in Stonington, Connecticut, recognized my teaching and wrote a feature article on my teaching skills.

Two close family friends have contributed to this book. Professor Bennie Wilson took time out of his busy schedule to review the manuscript. And a warm thank you to Dr. Charles Henry. For 42 years, I have watched you blossom. What a joy to have you write the biographical sketch of my life.

Another good friend is Peter Kessler, Senior Writer at *Golf Magazine;* we have developed a great working relationship that I cherish. Lorin Anderson, *Golf Magazine* Managing Editor (Instruction), has a keen eye for talent and introduced me to freelance writer Mark Gearen. Mark was essential in helping to deliver the book you now hold in your hands. He did much more than put words on a page—he captured the essence of my teaching concept and for that, I am eternally grateful.

Where would a teacher be without the students who learn, grow, and provide the personal gratification that makes it all worthwhile? Leslie Duke is a great friend and accomplished instructor. Two aspiring students whom I mentored, Robin Aikens and Darlene Stowers, have continued to excel, in the golf world and in their personal lives. A special thanks to another of my most promising students, Michael Freeman, who posed for the pictures in this book.

Adele Hodge, a writer and photographer, prepared me for my photo shoot for this book. The San Antonio Golf Club managers and staff have been fantastic. Trent Palmer, Director of The Golf Clubs of Texas, agreed to have our photo shoot at his facility. Doug Borow, Director of Olympia Hills Golf & Conference Center, and Tim Spurlock, Director, at the Bandit Golf Course, sanctioned my teaching at their courses.

Sometimes, friendship is what is needed most. Colonel (Ret.) Virgil Starkes and his wife, Sandra, welcomed me to San Antonio, Texas with open arms. Also, Matt Scherer, freelance reporter for the San Antonio *Express-News,* whose wonderful article literally introduced me to San Antonio. I cherish the thoughtful insights of my *Wedge Club Buddies* of Columbus, Ohio: Drs. Samuel Dixon and David Hamlar. Like my own son, Cal Richardson has been very special, assisting in the reading and editing of the manuscript and just being supportive. Ben Scott and I have spent many hours discussing golf theories and concepts into the wee hours of the morning. Thank you, Ben, knowing you is a blessing and my life is better because of you. Hurry up and retire so you can begin your second career in golf.

Thanks to my publisher, Jake Warde, of Warde Publishers, for bringing this book to its final form.

Finally, I have drawn inspiration from Dr. George Washington Carver. Having grown up as a young black man during the *Jim Crow* era, I know all too well how hard it was for people of color to advance in any profession. To gain the attention of the world, you had to, as Dr. Carver said, "do the common things of life in an uncommon way."

—Julius Richardson

Almost all the names I would mention have already been cited by Julius, but I wanted to add a few more words of emphasis from a writer's perspective.

Thanks first to Lorin Anderson of *Golf Magazine* for bringing us together. Thanks to Margaret Richardson for her patience and courtesy. Thanks for the support and help of my own family, especially my brother John.

Special thanks to Dr. Sam Dixon, who was the first to look over the manuscript and give us very helpful insights on it.

To those of Julius' pupils who described for me specific changes Julius made in their games, especially: Ms. Darlene Stowers, Delbert Smith, Charles Overstreet, Dr. Michael Whitmore, Jack Marbury, Robert Cude, Chris Thompson, Colonel (Ret.) Benny Wilson, Dr. David Hamlar, and Ms. Aleta Young.

To golf teacher Ben Jackson, whose assessment of Julius' teaching style was very helpful. To members of the USGTF already cited, who gave helpful accounts of how Julius taught and advised other instructors at their facility.

To Michael Freeman for his patience during the photography. To artist Phil Franke for his timely and skillful work on the illustrations.

To Virgil Starkes for frequent help along the way. To Ben Scott for editorial advice, and for his wisdom and counsel at several important junctures.

To teacher Wally Armstrong for connecting us to publisher Jake Warde, and to Jake for his work and understanding developing the project.

—*Mark Gearen*

Chapter 1
A New Way of Learning

My students have been telling me for years that I should write a book of golf instruction, and I'm delighted to have finally done so. I didn't write it for monetary gain, although I'll accept that, gladly. I wrote it because I believe I have something important to contribute to golf teaching.

It has long been my opinion that *golf is taught the wrong way.* I'd like to show a better path to good golf than the one most golfers are taking.

It's common for me to take an 18-handicapper, for instance, and help him or her get to a 10 or so after only six lessons in the space of three months. I have taken absolute beginners and in four months had them breaking 90, provided they worked at it.

The key to the dramatic improvement we achieve is a different approach to learning. I teach golf in the established way that we successfully teach other physical skills—in the military, for instance. Unfortunately, that way of teaching physical skills is *not used by the vast majority of golf teachers.* I believe over 90 percent of the attempted teaching and learning done in golf is completely ineffective.

Most golfers would admit this. At least they would ruefully admit that their own golf is cyclical—it gets a little better, gets a little worse, a little better, a little worse. It doesn't seem to advance.

1

When I walk along the line at the average driving range, in my estimation only about 2 percent of those hitting balls are improving by what they're doing. That's correct—one in fifty. Ninety-eight percent are either staying the same, or getting worse. It's an enormous waste of effort, which is why I often intervene.

The key is to learn to play golf the way we learn other physical skills.

Think about the physical skills we learn during our lives: Tying our shoelaces. Swimming. Driving a car. Playing football, soccer, and other team sports. Playing a piano. Riding a bicycle. Typing on a typewriter or computer. Boxing. Scuba diving. Flying an airplane. Sailing a sailboat. We seem determined to teach all these physical skills *one* way, and golf *another* way. My question is, why is golf taught differently?

I learned many of my physical skills in the military, where the result of learning something badly might be death. That changes one's attitude toward learning.

Teach a person to play card tricks—that is one thing. Teach a person to parachute from a plane—entirely another thing. The learning process changes from hit-or-miss casual to extremely focused and purposeful. And the method of teaching changes.

When danger is involved . . .

The way I teach is to apply this more stringent method to learning golf, even though there is no physical danger.

How *do* we teach a skill when there is an element of danger? Look at the teaching of parachuting, scuba diving, and flying an airplane, and you'll see there's a pattern to it.

First, we break the skill down into its component parts and teach those individually in a concentrated form. We begin with the simple, making sure we master each stage

... we learn skills more carefully.

before moving on. We use as many drills as possible to teach each aspect of the component part, drilling and drilling and drilling. While this goes on, the student is protected from what would normally be the consequences of his mistakes. For instance, the prep work for scuba diving is done on dry land. Only when a requisite skill level is reached do student and teacher get into the water.

Our teaching of golf should follow the same pattern. It isn't a matter of physical danger. But it *is* a matter of lifelong enjoyment or lifelong non-enjoyment of golf. Frankly, the joy of playing golf well is so extreme, and the drudgery of playing golf badly is so extreme, that golf is worth treating as if it were a skill involving danger.

That's the pattern of my teaching: breaking the skill into component parts, proceeding from the simple to the more complex, drilling until skilled, then reassembling.

While this goes on, we remove players from what would normally be the consequences of their actions (often by removing the club and ball entirely), until they are sufficiently skilled to get *positive results* from the beginning.

Only after this training are the club and ball re-introduced for full shots—and the results are wonderful.

It sometimes takes repeated discussions to convince players that my way is the way to go. But the rewards are worth it.

In truth, when I started teaching golf in the 1950s and '60s, I did it in the traditional way. I had players hit a batch of practice balls while I watched, I gave them some commentary on their swing, some encouragement, some "swing thoughts" to work on, and I sent them off.

I thought I was doing them good. I had been a scratch player. I knew the game. But from my perspective today, *I didn't know how to teach.*

It wasn't until I had taught for a few years that I stepped back and said, "wait a minute, something is wrong here." I began to reconsider, think about how I had learned other physical skills, think about the learning process itself. That's when my golf teaching began to change—and evolved eventually into what it is now.

Why This Method?

My method of teaching golf has proved extremely successful over the last 20 years. But mine is certainly not the only way to teach successfully.

For example, my friend Wally Armstrong uses physical devices to give players a feeling for a good swing.

Some teachers focus on the club and what the player should do with it, rather than the player's body. Teaching legend Ernest Jones taught very successfully that way, and so do Manuel de la Torre and his disciples today.

Teaching great John Jacobs teaches players to work backward from ball flight to understand their swing patterns—this can be a very effective technique.

So it's possible to be a successful teacher using any of a number of techniques. But in promoting my own, I would say that, since changing to this style 20 years ago, I've had overwhelming success with players and a retention rate that has climbed every year.

There are other telltale signs that my system works. Here are some of them:

- My students start to hit the ball much straighter—their shot dispersion narrows. In particular, they don't slice the ball.

They might push the shot or pull it slightly, but once they are working with me, the wide slice disappears.

- Almost every golfer I've ever taught has reported that I improved his or her short game, often dramatically.

- After five lessons or so my students have acquired such a clear idea of the body angles and positions that produce good golf that they are able to give lessons to others, including players somewhat better than themselves.

- I'm able to work with players who have less power, less coordination, or less athleticism, and give them satisfaction playing golf. Even if you can hit the ball only 150 yards, as long as you hit it squarely, keep it in play, and learn a good short game, you're going to have fun.

- I'm able to help players eradicate longstanding bad habits. I constantly hear the comment, "Julius, now I finally know what my problem has been this last 20 years."

So, it's true mine isn't the only way. But I think these positive results are sufficient reason to give my method a thorough try.

For equipment you will need only the simple objects I use in teaching—a few clubs, a full length mirror (if possible it is worth investing in this), a length of string to make a putting station, a clothes hanger, three balls for use in the short game, and dowels or broken shafted clubs if you can come by them.

The first step is to understand my method and how it works.

The Pattern of My Lessons

The form of my golf lessons is quite different from the norm. Most teachers give lessons that last 30 minutes, and feature the striking of perhaps 30 or 40 balls, with intervals where the teacher makes suggestions and corrections, and gives the player "tips" or "things to work on."

My lessons last between 60 and 90 minutes, and there is little striking of balls. I have the player demonstrate his or her hold of the club, stance at the ball, alignment and posture, and may have the player hit three or four balls for diagnosis. By then I've assessed the player's game and we get down to work.

Although I tailor my teaching to each individual, what I teach *all* pupils is a course in "cumulative skills learning," much of it executed *without a club and ball.* I don't give the student "tips" to work on. I give instead an enjoyable "obstacle course" of drills designed to habituate certain postural angles and alignments. As I make clear, *it is the golf student's responsibility* to carry out the habituating process, through the assigned "homework" of drills.

I tell each player that I am the sort of teacher who turns the student into his or her own teacher. Golf students always like that idea.

As I explain, *it is impossible to teach a person the "feel" of a physical skill.* You can only put the person in position to teach himself or herself. The key to my success as a teacher is that *I know how to put the pupil in that position.*

Over many years of study, I have subdivided and subdivided the skills of golf into "bite-sized" parts, each assimilated through drill. These parts are cumulative. They build on each other, from the 1-foot putt through the drive; from the correct grip, stance, posture and alignment, through the swinging of the club.

My lessons last longer partly because *I send the player through a learning experience within the lesson.* And it's marvelous, when I do this, how players respond by getting into "their own little world," and doing an excellent job with the learning.

My teaching strongly emphasizes the pre-swing skills. Golf's most astute commentators, such as Jack Nicklaus, legendary teacher John Jacobs, and five-time British Open winner Peter Thomson—

have said that the best golf instruction is "front loaded." That is, the more attention we pay to the pre-swing skills, the less trouble we will have with the swing itself. I agree 100 percent, which is why I have broken down these skills to a greater extent than any teacher I know of.

Fortunately, as a reader of this book, you'll be a recipient of that knowledge—so we will accomplish tremendous things for your game, before you ever draw the club back.

My favorite of all golf instructors was an Englishman named Percy Boomer, who taught in France from the 1920s through the 1940s. In his book *On Learning Golf* he did what golf pros and golf writers should have been doing for the last hundred years, only they haven't. He turned the spotlight away from the mechanics of the swing and onto the *learning process itself.*

It's the best move a golf teacher can make, because it opens doors for the student that cannot be opened merely by passing on technical information.

For instance, how does a good golfer learn the feel of a good golf swing? For many it's a case of trial and error or long practice, but is there a way to accelerate the process?

Helping Players Teach Themselves

As a teacher, I want to give my students a feel for the swing. But feel is elusive.

One of the first things one discovers as a teacher is that each golfer feels the swing differently. For this reason it is impossible as a teacher to describe your feeling for the swing and have a student acquire that feeling from your description. Yet there is no doubt that "feel" is what we are trying to convey. How can we do it?

One solution is that of Percy Boomer, who used imagery—like the image of "swinging in a barrel." I'll go along with that, and I use some imagery in my teaching. But much more than through imagery,

I believe you teach feel by sending the student through a physical experience that instills that feel.

Let's say the feel of a good golf swing is like going through the Panama Canal. Until you've gone through the Canal, you don't know what it feels like. I can't give you a verbal description of the Panama Canal and make you understand it; I can't tell you what it felt like when I went through the Canal and make you understand it. But I can take a tugboat, push your boat up to the mouth of the Panama Canal, push you in, and let you go through the experience yourself.

That's what I'm doing when I give players drills to work with, then step away and let them become their own teachers. Increment by increment, I send them through a series of experiences whereby they teach themselves the fundamentals, and the feel of the fundamentals, piece by piece. And I have sequenced these skills so that they build on each other, from the simplest skills to the complete game. I tell players, "I am going to send your game through a process of intelligent evolution."

How to Get Skill Inside a Golfer

If you want to play better golf, it's important to understand *how* golfers learn when they learn successfully.

I can't tell you how many times I have shared a lesson tee with another pro, looked over for a moment to watch him teach, and realized very well that this lesson was not going to "take."

The tragedy of golf teaching is the well-intended lesson that results in *no learning at all.* If you understand why this happens, you'll know how to make your own lessons succeed.

The Lesson That Fails—and Why Here's an example of a failed lesson. Let's say you have a young pro who plays well, understands swing mechanics and truly cares about his pupil's improvement.

The student hits a few balls for diagnosis, and it's clear his

| Figure 1.1   Open Shoulders | Figure 1.2   Square Shoulders |

address is flawed (Figure 1.1). The shoulders are too open and the chin is too low. The pro realizes this is blocking the player's development.

So the pro tells the player to address the ball, then the pro steps up and puts everything in proper position, leaving the pupil in a perfect address (Figure 1.2). Then he allows the player to strike the shot.

This process is repeated perhaps 20 times during the lesson. The player seems to be hitting the ball better and adopting the new address more and more automatically.

When the lesson time is up, the player is sent on his way.

My question to you is: What learning took place?

The answer is *zero*. Absolutely none.

Because here is what will happen the next time the student plays: He will try to adopt the new address, try to remember its details, he will hit a few good shots, but also some bad shots, and slowly, as the round progresses, he will *revert back to his old address.*

Teacher and pupil were operating in good faith. But neither understood *how to get a golf skill inside a golfer, and make it stay there.*

How do you do that?

It's a little like getting a ship inside a bottle.

I'm sure you've seen model ships like the one in Figure 1.3. How does the ship get inside the bottle?

Can you get a model ship inside a bottle by cramming the whole ship into the bottle? It may be the most obvious way to try to do it. But you can't do it that way (Figure 1.4).

How do you get the ship into the bottle? The answer is, *you dismantle it.* Draw in the yardarms, take down the mast, slip the ship inside, straighten the mast, spread the yardarms, and there you are (Figure 1.5).

How do you get skill inside a golfer? *You dismantle it.*

The pro whose lesson I just described failed because he never broke down the skill.

Figure 1.3

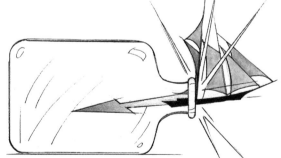

Figure 1.4

Better Golf: A Skill Building Approach

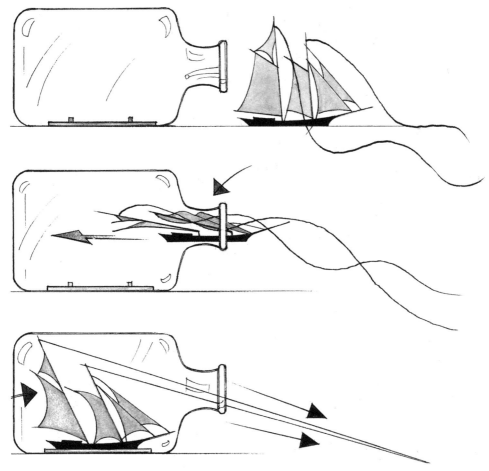

Figure 1.5

In effect, the pro was like someone trying to get a model ship inside a bottle by cramming the whole ship inside the bottle.

In golf, giving the student all the elements of a good address at the same time may be the most obvious way to try to teach him. But you can't do it that way.

Instead you must dismantle the good address—split it into its parts, its sub-skills, so to speak—get the sub-skills inside the golfer one at a time, then reassemble.

To accomplish this, I give the player drills to work on getting the chin well up—*nothing else.* Then I give the player drills to work on his spine tilt—*nothing else.* Then drills to work on his shoulder alignment—*nothing else.*

Gradually we drill our way through the sub-skills of a good address. All this time the player *isn't hitting balls,* isn't even addressing a ball, because he or she doesn't need to, and because it will only detract from the learning. But, in effect, it's as if we are dismantling the ship and getting it inside the bottle. At the end of the training, the golfer's subconscious "reassembles the ship," the golfer finds that he or she can step up to a golf ball and get into a superb address position with perfect alignment and posture, and it is a *habit.* That is how to get a golf skill inside a golfer—and make it stay there.

From Short Shots to Long Shots

In my teaching, we begin with short shots and advance to longer ones. I feel as if I must defend this method, because it has been attacked in the past—in fact, one of the attackers was Jack Nicklaus—so I feel I have some explaining to do.

The comment Nicklaus made in one of his books was that when golfers started with short shots and emphasized accuracy, it tended to limit their distance. They grew into players who, in Nicklaus's words, "bunted the ball down the fairway."

There was a time when Nicklaus had a point, because golf teachers, during the time Jack was coming up, generally based their instruction on *limiting movement,* "keep the head down," "keep the head still," "keep the left arm stiff," "keep the right elbow glued to the side," etc.

But my own instruction, and modern instruction generally, is designed to *free up* the player, rather than limit his motion.

My key to giving the golfer power and freedom is to establish angles and alignments at address that encourage powerful coiling during the swing.

For that reason I can begin the player with putts and short shots and build from there, at each stage consolidating our gains—so we don't get "lost," or frustrated, or quit the game—and the result is that eventually we hit powerful shots with the driver, all the time feeling that this stroke is a "logical extension" of our chipping stroke.

That is *continuity* in teaching.

If you were teaching someone to swim, you would never begin by tossing the person into 6-foot ocean swells. But that is what we do in golf when we take a beginning player or a high handicapper and put a driver in his or her hands. This player has not yet built up the skills to gain control over this implement, and the compromises the player engages in, trying to *get* control, will distort the swing, and put a limit on the player's development.

Far better to give them a less challenging club, or better yet, *no club at all,* until good habits are ingrained. Then the step up to the power clubs will not be such an intimidating one. The player will take it in stride, keep the fundamentals going, and build a much better swing.

I recently read in a Wall Street Journal article by James Sterba that 3½ million people take up golf every year in the United States, but 3½ million quit, so the number of people playing remains about the same. I think it's mostly frustration from missed shots that causes the quitting. If those players had been taught from short shots to long shots, I believe they would have stayed with the game.

Chapter 2
Getting to the Core
of the Game

I have a two-pronged approach to getting to the core of scoring at golf: get the ball in play off the tee, and develop a tidy short game within 50 yards of the hole. Almost all the big numbers in golf come from wild tee shots or wasteful short game sequences.

The Two Essentials:
On the Fairway, Tidy Short Game

The ability to hit fairways comes from the proper body angles and alignment at address. With those factors and a good short game set in place, there is no limit to what you can achieve as a golfer. It's simply a matter of how much you're willing to work at it.

The hallmark of the long game is the ability to hit the ball straight. The hallmark of the short game is the ability to control your distance.

I explain these things to my students right away, and from the start I work to give them a solid short game and start working on their body angles and alignment. If they turn out to be long hitters or show a special flair for shotmaking, that's a bonus. But that's not the essential. The essential "infrastructure" is the two points I just mentioned, and everything else builds from that.

15

I teach plenty of male players who hit the ball 220 yards or less, plenty of female players who hit the ball 160 yards or less. But I give them the body angles and alignment, so they can hit the ball flush and straight; I get them in command of their games from 50 yards in, so they have no real weaknesses in that area—and their scores start to drop. Furthermore, they're well enough educated in these matters, so when they take up golf after a long layoff, they know exactly what they must do to get themselves sharp. They are in control of the game, rather than the game controlling them.

If you think along those lines, you will have the same advantage.

Delivering the Ball to the Fairway

How do we solve problem number one, getting the ball into the fairway?

With most players I find it is necessary to change their attitude about driving. To the handicap player, hitting a tee shot is not a very "planned" experience, certainly not in terms of posture and alignment. The player gets on the tee asking:

"Can I hit it 300 yards?"

"Can I outdrive everybody in my foursome?"

"Can I curve it around the dogleg?"

He views each tee shot as an individual climax of excitement. His blood pressure rises and rises until the moment of truth, when he swings like an uncontrolled whirligig, something like Figure 2.1.

And though the ball sometimes flies straight, it often peels off into the bushes or rough, and the player has to go chase it.

The player loves his golf, but he's not doing a very good job of getting control over his fate.

When players learn from me, they develop a different attitude about driving, and here it is:

First of all, take the long view. Don't get all excited about how hard you're going to hit an individual drive, whether you can cut off

Better Golf: A Skill Building Approach

Figure 2.1

Peter Thomson on Golf

Peter Thomson, five time British Open champion, was known for the ability to simplify good golf. He said, "a light, tender, sensitive touch is worth a ton of brawn." He also said the main problem of the average golfer was "he's not set up right," meaning that his body angles and alignments at address have him beaten before he begins.

I think those two statements summarize a great deal of my teaching. If my pupils learn good touch, and learn the body angles that get the ball onto the fairway, they have the basis for dramatically reducing their handicaps.

the dogleg, etc. Start thinking in terms of all 14 tee shots you're going to hit that day (not counting par 3s), and what you hope to achieve.

What you should want to do is hit the highest percentage of fairways you can, with power that is at least adequate. You're not trying to pound an individual tee shot a great distance. What you're trying to do is develop a *patented delivery motion,* almost like the patented delivery motion of a bowler. A motion that will put the ball in the fairway again and again and again.

A bowler doesn't get all excited about rolling the ball as fast as he can, or rolling this ball faster than the previous ball. He tries instead to roll each one with consistent speed, consistent rhythm, consistent control of his body angles (Photo 2.1).

What's the key to making this kind of delivery motion in golf? The answer is: *key angles in the posture and alignment of the body.*

When we maintain these angles, the effect is that, instead of trying to hit the ball with an uncontrolled motion through sheer eye-hand coordination, we make a much more consistent motion, no matter how sharp we feel that day, no matter what sort of golf hole we are playing. Even our "misses" tend to stay much straighter. Our shot dispersion becomes much narrower.

Getting those angles under control is much more important than swinging hard. During the time when we are adopting these angles, we may swing more slowly at first, because we're more self-conscious, which always slows down movement. But as we learn them,

Photo 2.1   Photo sequence from *Bowling Execution* by John Jowdy.

Better Golf: A Skill Building Approach

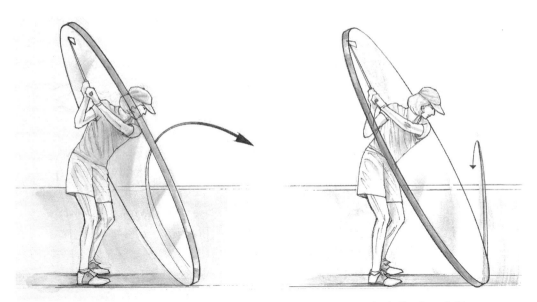

Figure 2.2   The drills in this book help change the slicer's "wipe across the ball" plane (left) to a square-striking plane (right) that results in straight shots.

our muscles relax, and we send the ball quite long, and down the fairway.

Another great side effect is that, if the player suffers from a cutting or slicing swing plane, adopting these address angles tends to adjust the plane into a straight striking plane (Figure 2.2). That's why many lifelong slicers find that they lose their slice while working with me. The result of these changes is that players hit fairways much more consistently, and when they do make errors, the errors are less severe.

The difference this approach makes in scoring is enormous. Remember, almost all the serious trouble in golf—stroke-and-distance penalties and so on—is *off the tee.* How often do you incur a stroke-and-distance penalty on an approach shot? Virtually never. Getting the ball in play is vitally important.

Take the long view of driving. Stop thinking, "can I hit it 300 yards?" Start thinking, "what do I need to do with my posture and alignment angles to make a consistent delivery motion?"

The more you think this way, the more you focus on the address position, and you see it as a golden opportunity to take control of your fate before you ever swing the club. Habituating good angles sets off a chain reaction of positive changes in your swing.

The Six Key Angles

We will learn six key angles to help us control our swing. As long as we have these angles properly in tune, it doesn't matter whether we're fat or thin, male or female, young or old, whether our swing is short or long, whether we're flexible or not so flexible, whether we hit our drive more than 300 yards or less than 200 yards—as long as these angles are properly maintained, we'll swing in a good plane and path, and strike the ball well.

But you can't just adopt these angles immediately upon seeing them. The way I teach golf, you "grow into them" by starting with the short game and drilling to learn these angles as the shots become longer. In this way your game becomes progressive, and at the same time the angles are firmly set.

The best way to visualize them is through schematic drawings.

Figure 2.3   Angle 1:
Spine Tilt Forward

Angle Number 1: Spine Tilt Forward

The first is the spine tilt (Figure 2.3). This is the angle of the spine at address, which is about 30 degrees from vertical, varying according to the individual—but the important thing is that it be maintained during the swing until the ball is struck.

The tendency of handicap golfers is to straighten up out of that angle during the

Figure 2.4   Angle 2:
Spine Tilt Away from the Target

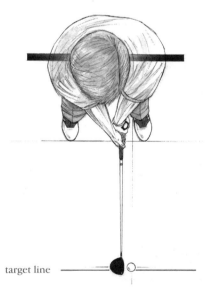

target line

Figure 2.5
Angle 3: Square Shoulders

swing. When they do, the stability of the swing disintegrates—it's like swinging a door while the hinges are getting loose from the jamb.

Angle Number 2: Spine Tilt Away from the Target

The second angle is a tilt of the spine away from the target at address (Figure 2.4). This tilt is crucial. It allows the right hand to get to its lower place on the shaft at address, while the shoulders remain in plane with the target line. But it achieves something else just as important. When the player sets his spine like this, it eliminates the "reverse pivot" before it can happen. (The reverse pivot is the body move in the swing where the torso leans toward the target during the backswing, away from the target in the through swing, with an insufficient movement of weight during the motion. It produces weak slices that lack distance.)

The proper spine tilt away from the target sets the player up for a powerful coil during the backswing and a powerful move onto the forward leg as he or she strikes.

Angle Number 3: Square Shoulders

The third angle is the alignment of the shoulders, *in plane with the target line,* as you see in Figure 2.5. The tendency among handicap golfers is to align the shoulders open to the target line. In fact, they jut the right shoulder forward to get the right hand to its lower place on the shaft. Squaring the shoulders, rather than aligning with them open, is a hugely important part of our technique.

Angle Number 4: Right Knee Angle

The fourth angle, the angle of the right knee (Figure 2.6), is important primarily because it helps us maintain the first angle, the spine angle. We want the right knee at a certain angle at address, and we need to maintain that angle during the backswing. Among handicap players, the tendency is to straighten this knee too much during the backswing, which causes the spine angle to straighten.

Figure 2.6
Angle 4: Right Knee Angle

Better Golf: A Skill Building Approach

incorrect angle   correct angle

Figure 2.7   Angle 5: Head and Chin Angles

Angle Number 5: Head and Chin Angle

The fifth angle is the posture of the head and chin, which must be very erect, with the chin well up and pointing to the right of the ball (Figure 2.7). The tendency of handicap golfers is to sink the chin into the chest with the nose pointing at the ball. This also causes a reverse pivot because the player can't coil properly—the chin is blocking his shoulders from turning.

Angle Number 6: Hinging Right Elbow

The last of our six angles is a changing or moving angle, the angle of the right elbow as we take the club into the backswing. As we do this, the right arm must be soft, and the right elbow must *hinge easily*, must not resist bending (Figure 2.8). When the elbow resists bending, a chain reaction occurs that causes the player's entire body to sway away from the target. Very few golfers understand how important this easy hinging of the right elbow is.

Figure 2.8   Angle 6: Hinging Right Elbow

There are our six angles. We will find that, if our hold of the club is correct and our arms are relaxed, we can allow these angles to control the direction of our swing. We can make the "patented delivery motion" I've talked about and hit the ball much straighter day in and day out.

Better Golf: A Skill Building Approach

As I will mention several times in this book, this is not an eye-hand coordination game, it is a skeleton position game. When we get our angles correct, we control the skeleton. When we control the skeleton, we control the swing.

Even given the above description of six angles, don't think for a moment that, by simply looking at them and understanding them, you've accomplished something for your game. You've accomplished nothing. You cannot go out tomorrow and use them as you play.

You can only adopt these angles over time, through patient repetition of drills.

Our Plan of Learning

I hope this introduction of key angles has whetted your appetite for things to come, and now we can get down to business.

The instruction in this book is divided into clearly defined sections, loosely based on my standard half dozen lessons.

Here's how we'll approach it:

Pre-Swing Skills

Our first lessons will be on the all-important pre-swing skills such as the hold of the club (both for putting and full shots), and the proper angles of the body.

After reading a given section it is essential that you *actually perform the drills described* and perform them repeatedly, even if you wonder whether they can really help you. If you truly want to advance, periods of drill must become a regular part of your routine.

Putting Mechanics and Putting Touch

After the pre-swing skills are mastered, I will present my lesson in putting mechanics, comprising five drills.

Boxed material like this throughout the book indicates skill-building drills. These are exercises which, if performed repeatedly, can form good habits, and get the player out of bad habits.

Golfers who practice these "skill builders" arrive at the course more prepared to make good swings, hit good shots, and get more pleasure from the game.

For convenience I use the word "drill" throughout the book, but I want you to think of these skill-building drills not as a chore, but as an opportunity to get more fun from your golf.

Some of these drills should be repeated as frequently as possible for the rest of your playing career—the ladder drill and certain postural drills, for example. But most only need to be repeated frequently when you are first reading about them—because at that point they serve as diagnostic tools. If your habits in a given area are already good, you won't need to repeat the drill much. If your habit is bad, that is where the drill must be repeated most persistently.

I'm often asked if there is a specific number of repetitions that will establish a given habit. This varies according to the individual—but students can usually tell when a habit is formed.

These drills help you build up your stroke, and begin the process of transferring trust to the subconscious, which must take place with all the learning in this book.

The last drill, the ladder drill for putting touch, will eventually become the focus of your entire short game. The ability to control how far we hit the ball, when we are within 50 yards of the hole, is one of the two great scoring attributes of golf—the other being the ability to hit the tee shot into the fairway.

After the sections on putting, you are to go through a period of gestation. Work with the drills, reread the material until the concepts make more and more sense to you. Changing your approach to golf is never easy or immediate, but it will be worth it.

Chipping and Short Pitching

The next chapter is on chipping and short pitching. I consider it essential that all students become fine chippers, not only for scoring, but because chipping is critical in the transition to full shotmaking.

To learn chipping most effectively, you must learn it *in steps,* as I teach it here. It is extremely important that you actually *go through those steps*. Start out from a square stance as instructed, and only later go to an open stance. Please realize that I have adopted this "step" program through long experience of what works—and that's true of all the step programs in this book.

Consolidating Our Gains

At certain stages along our way, I will remind you of what you are expected to learn, and what important "themes" will run through our learning from short shots to long shots.

For instance, we want to establish the habit of square shoulders at address from the beginning, even as you begin putting, and that "theme" will keep recurring as the shots get longer.

The Leap to the Full Shots, and How It Becomes Easier

After learning putting, chipping, and short wedge shots, instead of going straight on to learn full swings, we stop. We *don't* get into full swings yet but instead prepare extensively *before we allow ourselves to swing full.*

We learn perfect ball position and alignment, learn the pivot or body action of the swing, learn "connection" between arms and body, and rehearse the striking action of forearms, wrists and hands.

The full swing of a power club can be a very disorienting thing if we have not prepared properly. Most of the bad swing habits in golf are acquired because the player did *not* properly prepare before he or she began making a full swing.

Ball Position and Alignment—I have a very high standard for ball position and alignment, because it so strongly influences performance. As far as humanly possible, we want our body, the club, and the ball in the *exact* same positions relative to each other with a given club each time we address (assuming a level lie). This causes a tremendous improvement in consistency and accuracy.

The Pivot—For our preparation here, we don't hit shots or even hold a club. The best way to learn the pivot or body motion of the swing is to start with the greatest freedom of motion—not from golf posture but from a standup position—and adjust from there until we acquire the move we want. Then we learn to make that free motion within the confines of golf posture and alignment.

Again, this is a step process and there is a reason for it. If we had started with golf posture and alignment, we would have restricted our motion too much. But by "starting free"—then shaping and controlling "just enough"—we get our best performance.

"Connection" of Arms to Body—Our next step of preparing for full swings is to "connect" arm motion and body motion, keying particularly on the closeness of the upper left arm to the torso. Next, we work on the striking motion of the arms, forearms, hands, and club, and its coordination with body movement.

Once these things have been taken care of, we have done so much to make our motion correct that by the time we start striking full shots our success rate is tremendously high, much higher than if we had simply started out hitting the ball and tried to improve by trial and error.

The Full Swing

After working on all the skills just described the reader will be free to do what he or she has been longing to do all along—hit full shots!

But it is also important to go through the swing motion itself, to make sure our preparation has succeeded, and also review the instruction that got us there.

Checkpoints and Problem Solving—Our first step is a "walkthrough" of the swing, going from address to finish, along the way discussing where the club should be, what details in body position we need to check, and so on. I also provide drills to help with problems that tend to come up.

Final Review of the Six Key Angles—We next review, for the last time, the six angles we keyed on from the beginning, and which have become more and more important for your game, as the shots got longer. And we'll end with some final remarks about relaxation and how it helps your game.

This will conclude the physical instruction of the book. It will be followed by a chapter on the management of one's game and attitude, followed by some concluding remarks about this style of instruction and what I hope to contribute with this book.

I strongly suggest that you go through all the material, and perform each drill at least a few times as you read about it, and much more later. You will find that the drills serve a diagnostic function. If the drill feels awkward, you probably need work in that area. If the drill is done easily, you probably execute that fundamental skill quite well. So you can "feel your way forward" in terms of your own game.

If you are already a very skilled player—let's say a single-figure handicapper—you don't really need to start with putting and the short game unless you consider yours a weakness. You can feel free to go through the book and pick and choose what especially applies to you.

Chapter 3
Pre-Swing Skills

The first lesson I give in person covers a great deal of material, because I want the player to start habituating on several fronts. We cover: spine angle (both the inclination toward the ball and the inclination to the player's right, as he sees it); the hold of the club for full shotmaking; the hold of the club for putting; the "windshield wiper" drill of the hands and forearms to learn to rotate the club as we swing it in a full shot; a series of five drills to establish putting mechanics; and a sixth drill to learn putting "touch." We will cover this material in two chapters.

Spine Tilt Toward the Ball

Our object is to set the body in the best anatomical position for ball striking. This position includes several key body angles and alignments. We will habituate those without even striking a ball, simply by drill.

When you walk down the "firing line" on the practice tee at a PGA or LPGA tournament, you see nothing *but* this anatomically correct position.

Conversely, when you walk down the line at the average driving range, you virtually *never* see it. Instead you see chins stuck in

Figure 3.1   Correct spine angle   Incorrect spine angle

When proper spine angle is maintained (left) the club can be swung in the proper plane. When the player straightens up out of the proper spine angle (right), the body loses its plane of movement, like a door that has come off its hinges, and the path of the club also gets off plane.

chests, shoulders wide open to the target line, knee flex that is either "way too much" or "not at all"—nothing but postural mistakes. These mistakes are the "glass ceiling" preventing these players from reaching a better level.

Spine angle is the prime angle in all of golf. It's the first thing I teach, even before the hold of the club. Again, when the handicap golfer straightens up out of the spine angle during the swing, the stability of the posture disintegrates—like a door with the hinges coming loose as in Figure 3.1.

32   *Better Golf: A Skill Building Approach*

When I start the pupil out, I always assist with Spine Angle Drill 1. I like to place a mirror to our right—approximately where the camera was for these shots. I make the angle, have the subject flex his knees, remove the club and let him drop his arms into the address position. At each of these steps we can look to our right, and check progress in the mirror.

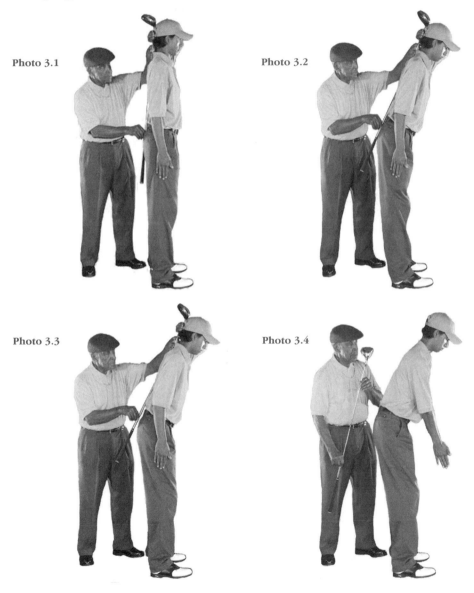

Photo 3.1

Photo 3.2

Photo 3.3

Photo 3.4

You are now ready to perform drill number one yourself. If you are doing this at home, it's a great advantage to have a mirror to your right, so you can check on the angles being formed.

Place the club on your back as shown in Photo 3.5. It touches the body at the upper back in the thoracic region, and at the buttocks. There will be a slight hollow above the buttocks where the body is not flat to the club. The depth of this hollow will depend on your build.

From this straight-up position, bend from the pelvic area, while keeping the club against the body (Photo 3.6), then flex the knees slightly (Photo 3.7).

The head remains in its normal relation to the torso. Do not bend your head back in order to touch it to the club.

Also, avoid the tendency to draw the buttocks in when you flex the knees—be careful to keep the buttocks out.

Photo 3.5

Photo 3.6

Photo 3.7

Stand straight up, holding a club against your waist as shown in Photo 3.8.

Bend from the pelvic area, sticking your buttocks out (Photo 3.9), then flex your knees slightly, keeping your back as straight as it was in drill number 1 (Photo 3.10).

Photo 3.8

Photo 3.9

Photo 3.10

This drill is my favorite for spine angle, but it demands more balance and strength than the first two. For some players, particularly seniors or those with balance problems, we make modifications, as I will describe.

Start from an upright position facing straight forward with the feet together (Photo 3.11). Lift one of your feet—start with the right one—and move it behind you as indicated in Photo 3.12. You should find yourself standing entirely on your left leg, with your right leg well out behind you and straight, and your trunk and right leg forming almost a straight line, as the photo shows. *This automatically sets your spine at the proper angle for golf.*

Without changing that angle, and keeping the buttocks "sticking out," bring the right foot forward and place it on the ground next to your left foot (Photo 3.13).

Don't pull the buttocks back in when you do so! This is a mistake players constantly make—use a mirror to check on this.

Once you have brought your feet together, step with the left foot 4 inches to the left, then step to the right with the right foot to spread the stance (Photo 3.14).

Perform this drill constantly, until assuming the proper angles becomes natural to you. And remember that even though the angles are sharply defined, it's always important that the body be *relaxed!*

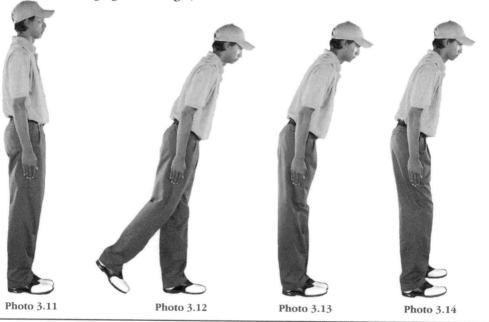

Photo 3.11   Photo 3.12   Photo 3.13   Photo 3.14

It is also extremely helpful to perform this drill while propping your chin well *up* with your forefinger or middle finger, as shown in Photo 3.15. In addition to being well up, the chin should point to the right of the imaginary ball, which helps your coil and prevents a reverse pivot.

Some players will have trouble with their balance when standing on one leg. If that is so for you, use a club like a cane as shown in Photo 3.16.

Photo 3.15   Photo 3.16

Spine Angle Drill 3 is the best of the three drills for learning the proper tilt toward the ball, and should be practiced constantly until the tilt, and the slight flex of the knees, become second nature. For those who tend to slump at address, it will take a good deal of work and a good deal of self-checking using a mirror.

The other aspect of spine angle that must be learned besides the inclination toward the ball, is the inclination to the player's right. We'll get to that in a moment.

Incidentally I'm sometimes asked why I give three or four drills to achieve a certain skill or fundamental, rather than just one drill. The answer is that everyone feels the swing differently, and even feels these drills differently. One drill will "strike a chord" with a given player, another won't. So the best way is to give you several to work from, and have you select a favorite.

Spine Tilt to the Player's Right

Next we learn the other part of spine angle—the slight inclination away from the target. This tilt achieves two important objectives: First, it allows the right hand to reach its lower place on the shaft while the shoulders remain in plane with the target line. Second, it puts the body in position to coil powerfully during the backswing without "reverse pivoting."

Again, the reverse pivot is a body motion during the swing where the torso leans toward the target during the backswing, and away from the target during the forward swing. It causes weak shots to the right and a lack of power.

I've been using the Grandfather Clock Drill on page 39 for many years, but lately I've discovered an alternate that has been even more effective in giving players a vivid feel for this subtle, but crucial, tilt of the body—namely the Airplane Drill on page 40.

All of these spine tilt drills should be practiced a *very* great deal, until the two spine angles become automatic. It's often necessary to undo bad habits, because most players start out with the classic duffer's posture: spine *not* tilted away from the target, right shoulder forward and the shoulder alignment wide open, right arm riding high, right arm tense, chin stuck in the chest. From this position it is almost impossible to do anything but slice the ball.

I tell players that when they have a bad habit—usually an address habit—it is like a scratch in a record. It will always be there—our subconscious never completely forgets the habits we have absorbed—but if we learn the good habit through drills that we repeat and repeat, gradually the bad habit is superseded by the new "groove" we are creating.

Stand upright facing forward, holding a driver in one hand, the butt of the club against your chin—see photo 3.17. The shaft of the club is vertical.

Next, bend forward from the pelvic area and flex the knees (Photo 3.18). The low end of the club should be about midway between your legs.

Next, tilt your spine just enough so that the clubhead moves 3 or 4 inches to your left and bumps your left leg (Photo 3.19). This gives you the essential tilt you need.

If you like, you can keep your body in that position, let go of the club, let it fall to the ground, and lower your arms into the address position.

Be careful to accomplish this "bump" via a tilt of the spine away from the target, setting the right shoulder lower than the left, rather than thrusting the right shoulder forward—which is the wrong way to do it.

You could call this the grandfather clock drill, because the club moves like the stroke of a grandfather clock.

Photo 3.17

Photo 3.18

Photo 3.19

Stand erect with your arms straight out in the form of a T like the wings of an aircraft (Photo 3.20).

Next, tilt your spine to your right as if you are gently banking the aircraft. The tips of your right fingers will be lowered by about 8 to 10 inches (Photo 3.21). *Notice that with your arms outstretched, you can feel the tilt of your spine much more vividly.*

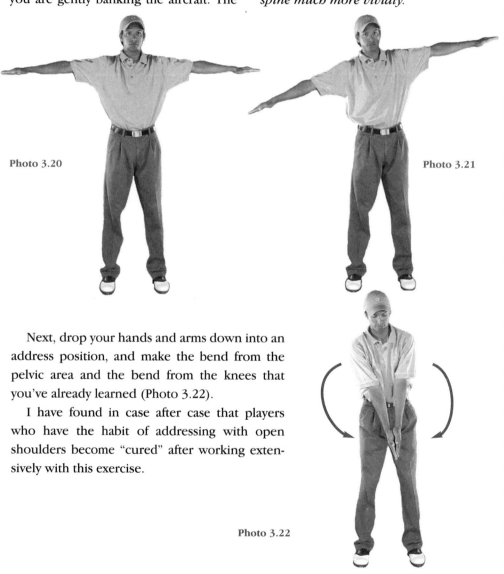

Photo 3.20

Photo 3.21

Next, drop your hands and arms down into an address position, and make the bend from the pelvic area and the bend from the knees that you've already learned (Photo 3.22).

I have found in case after case that players who have the habit of addressing with open shoulders become "cured" after working extensively with this exercise.

Photo 3.22

The bad habit will reappear once in awhile, and we should expect that and not be upset by it. For the most part, we succeed in establishing a new habit that will make us much better players.

Well-Defined Postural Angles

Keeping your angles "sharp" or well-defined at address is very important. It helps you maintain the proper plane during the swing, and helps you coil more easily. Tiger Woods at address shows those sharply defined angles. Mike Weir of Canada, 2003 Masters winner, is a left-hander with superb postural angles. Michelle Wie shows excellent angles.

Look in a mirror and see how sharp and well-defined your own angles are.

Players who simply "relax into it" at address—often with slightly slumped shoulders and ill-defined angles—tend to play very much by feel and eye-hand coordination. They play well on their home courses, or courses they're comfortable on. When they play on strange courses, they don't do as well. On extra tough courses, they don't do as well.

A good example of a player who "relaxes into it" is Colin Montgomerie. And I admit that he has had a great career, plays strange courses well, and all the rest of it. But in my opinion he succeeds because of overwhelming talent and an early exposure to the game—not because of his posture. I'd much prefer that you use Woods or Weir for a model and work on all the drills described in this book. Make all the angles sharply defined, but *keep the body relaxed.* Mirror work helps with this (see the next page).

The Hold of the Club

Our next step is to work on our hold of the club. But first of all, it would be a very good idea if, before working on your hold of the

I'm a strong believer in "mirror work" to check on body angles and alignments.

I recently drove out to a lesson with a socially-connected woman student. I was holding my practice mirror on the cart. She asked why I used the mirror, rather than the video equipment other pros use.

I said, "Imagine you and your husband are going to the biggest social event of the season. You want your face and hair to be perfect. In your home you have the most expensive video system, the best Polaroid camera, the best digital camera, and your mirror. Which would you trust?"

"The mirror."

Case closed. The image is bigger, clearer, and more detailed. The only negative is that the right-handed golfer sees himself left-handed, and vice versa. But if you know what to look for, it doesn't matter.

You're looking at the right knee, the left shoulder, or some other single detail I've told you is pertinent.

I regret to say that video is having some unfortunate effects. Often the bad player takes one look and gets discouraged. He thought he looked like Gene Littler with a golf club, and he looks like Lon Chaney with a golf club. In reality he can be improved quickly, but he sees only the negative, and his self-esteem drops -- the teacher loses a student who might have become a good player.

I think the mirror works much better.

club, you spent a week on spine angle, performing 30 repetitions of each drill a day. That's the sort of persistent, committed practice I'm talking about, and that's the sort of *separation of one skill from another* in the learning of the skills, that causes accelerated learning.

Now about the hold of the club: I prefer the expression "hold of the club" rather than "grip," which can be an unfortunate word in the minds of golfers.

People associate the word "grip" with clenching an object between the thumb and the palm of the hand, as when we grip a rope for a tug of war. However, when we hold a golf club like that, we swing the club in a stiff, wooden manner, without much clubhead speed.

We must learn that if we want to be a good golfer, our hands are used a little differently from how they're used in daily life, and it's instructive to note two differences:

First, in daily life, when we hold something intending to swing it to hit something else (as with a tennis racket, tack hammer, sledge-hammer, etc.), we maintain a secure hold of it by using our thumb to wedge it against the palm of our hand.

In golf, the implement is held primarily by the fingers, and the thumbs are subordinated, they are no longer the primary holders.

Second, in daily life, the right hand of a right-hander (or left hand of a left hander) has a very dominant function, and when we want something done, it just "goes there." When we want something struck with an implement, the dominant hand just "moves it there."

In golf, we cannot allow our dominant hand to simply "take charge" in this fashion, because if it does, there will be a flip of the hands forward, and this is one of the worst things in golf. It mistimes swings. It destroys short game shots.

So there are natural impulses we must overcome, to train the hands to become "golfing hands."

When we adopt a proper hold, where the thumb does not clench, and where the club is secured primarily in the fingers, we may feel at first that we are not in control of the club. But eventually

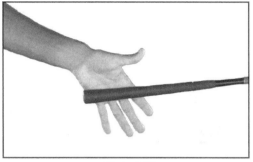 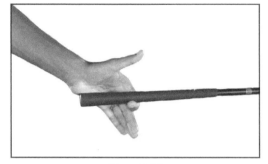

Photo 3.23   Photo 3.24

we get used to it, and swing much more fluidly and with greater clubhead speed.

First, then, we learn the proper position of the hands on the club.

Photo 3.23 shows how the left hand should be positioned. The opened left hand shows where the club passes diagonally from the second joint of the forefinger to the base of the little finger.

When the left hand is closed on the club, the butt of the club is wedged below the pad of the left palm. Photo 3.24 shows how the club can be held by the pad and forefinger alone—this is a good test of whether it's snugged under the pad.

Once the grip is completed, from the player's vantage point at address, the left thumb should be slightly on the right side of the shaft, not on the top of the shaft. We want to establish and maintain an adherence between the thumb and the part of the hand just below the base of the forefinger. If you have very small hands and have trouble feeling control with this adherence, we'll allow a little separation. If this is a problem, you should consider being refitted for smaller grips.

Next we place the right hand on the club and, again, hold the club primarily in the fingers. I teach players the overlapping grip or Vardon grip (Photo 3.25), in which the little finger of the right hand is placed between the forefinger and middle finger of the left hand,

Better Golf: A Skill Building Approach

Photo 3.25 Overlapping   Photo 3.26 Interlocking   Photo 3.27 Ten-finger

as shown. There is a tradition that the interlocking (Photo 3.26) and the ten-finger (Photo 3.27) grips can help players with small hands, but I have found that the overlapping grip works best for the vast majority.

As mentioned, it is essential to become comfortable holding the club in the fingers. To achieve this, work with the "finger curls" and "holding tees" drills described on the next pages—as you practice these, particularly if you are a middle- or upper-handicapper, you will find that you're holding the club more in the fingers, with less clinching.

To demonstrate where the club fits in your hand when you have achieved a good finger hold, make a "finger curl" with your right hand, your palm facing you, then place the forefinger of your left hand inside the "hollow" created by the curled fingers of the right hand. That's how the grip of the club will fit snugly in.

It is also important to acquire the ability to rotate the club as you swing it, with the back of the left hand in line with the left forearm. The rotational drills will help you achieve that.

To learn to trust your hold of the club in your fingers, practice "finger curls." Simply hold your hands out with the fingers straight (Photo 3.28), then bend the fingers from the middle knuckles to curl into a grip (Photo 3.29), then go back to straight again.

Just five minutes of these exercises a day can help you obtain the habit of a proper finger hold.

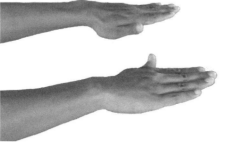

Photo 3.28

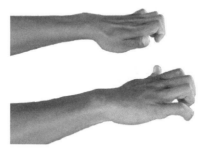

Photo 3.29

The Significance of Finger Curls

Most golfers don't quite understand what is being accomplished by the finger curl and "holding tees" exercises. You may think they are trivial, because the muscles and joints involved are so small.

But if you are a player who holds the club too much in the palms, these drills will make a great difference in how fluid your swing is, and how quickly you can swing the club.

The first great player to show what could be accomplished with this type of hold was Harry Vardon, who dominated European golf from the 1890s until the First World War. Since that time, low handicap and scratch golfers have used a finger hold almost exclusively— you rarely see a good player with a "palmy" grip. Among middle and upper handicappers, you see the club held much more in the palms—which tells you something.

When they first change to a finger hold, players tend to feel a lack of control, especially if they have played many years with their old grip. These drills are a great help making the change. The more time spent performing them, at any time during the day, the better.

This drill trains you to get the base of the thumb adhering to the base of the forefinger of each hand. It isn't enough to tell you to do it, you must get in the habit.

Start off by placing golf tees, or even leaves of grass, in the hollow between the base of your thumb and the base of your forefinger, as shown in Photo 3.30, and keep them there for extended periods, on the golf course and off it.

Photo 3.30

Are you planning to watch a baseball game or a sitcom this evening? During that time you can put a golf tee between the thumb and forefinger of each hand, and perform finger curls at intervals. All of that will help your golf.

If you are a middle- or high-handicapper, it won't be long before your hands operate in a completely different way when holding a club.

I encourage my players to develop the attitude that *every bit of effort directed at habituation helps their golf,* so they can always be working on their games.

Arm Rotation

The next two skills we work on are your ability to rotate the club as you swing it, and your ability to relax your arms while holding and swinging the club. These are essential preparations for improving your long game.

Most golfers who come to me have some golfing experience, but they are not satisfied with their games, and the chief trouble with their full shots is usually slicing. As they learn from me and perform the requested drills, they find that they are no longer "wiping" across the ball, but instead are swinging from the inside, to the ball, back to the inside.

But the player making this change from a slicing plane to a square striking plane must learn to rotate the club as he or she swings it, instead of using the "wipe across" hand and wrist motion that the slicer uses.

This preparation begins long before we ever hit full shots, and I have found over many years of experience that the earlier I prepare the player in this way, the better for his or her development.

We learn this through the "windshield wiper" or rotational drill, first performed without a club, then with a club.

Hold your hands in front of you in a "prayer" position, palm to palm and fingers extended (Photo 3.31). Use your forearms and arms to rotate your hands clockwise until the back of the left hand faces upward (Photo 3.32), then counterclockwise until the back of the right hand faces upward (Photo 3.33).

Photo 3.31

Photo 3.32

Photo 3.33

Hold a club in your golf grip, in front of you so that the club shaft is vertical, as in Photo 3.34. Rotate the hands and forearms in the same way clockwise until the back of the left hand faces upward (as does the face of the club), see Photo 3.35. Then rotate in the other direction until the back of the right hand (and the back of the clubhead) faces upward (Photo 3.36). The motion is similar to that of a windshield wiper, but at only about one-third the speed of a windshield wiper.

It is absolutely essential that the back of your left hand remains in line with the forearm during this exercise —monitor this constantly.

At first some players may not be strong enough to perform this drill holding the club at the very end. If you have this problem, it's best to begin by choking up on the club almost to the metal (or graphite), if necessary, until you're accustomed to the exercise and feel you can hold the club farther out.

From the first lesson that I teach, players perform this all-important exercise daily. It is crucially important to develop this rotational ability from the beginning. It will not be relevant as we work our way through the short game. But it prepares you for the future, particularly if you tend to slice.

Photo 3.34   Photo 3.35   Photo 3.36

Arm Relaxation

Arm relaxation is critical for a simple reason: If the hold of the club is proper, and the arms are truly relaxed, we don't need to worry about the motion of our hands and wrists. We can act as if "the hands are the clubface." That is, we can swing with the triangle of our arms and shoulders, keeping the hands and wrists passive—and the clubface will tend to "true up" at contact.

So arm relaxation is extremely desirable, but for many golfers difficult to achieve. Players themselves may not know they have a problem. In some areas of golf there is a wide gap between what the player perceives is happening and what really is. Arm tension is one of those areas.

Players will swear up and down that their arms are relaxed, but as a teacher I take one look and realize they are in "clinch mode."

I say that I want their arms as relaxed as wet noodles, and I can usually prove that they're "not there yet" by using the "arms pulled away" drill, and the "club at 45°" drill on the following pages.

Relaxation of the arms is essential. One of the best shotmakers ever on tour was Jimmy Demaret, who won the Masters three times, plus about 30 other tournaments. When Demaret played, he would often shake his arms to loosen them, as if trying to shake water from his fingers. Do that, and you'll sense how relaxed your arms become. You're like a baseball pitcher loosening his arm between pitches. When you take hold of a club, don't let that relaxation be replaced by tension.

First, the player stands in front of me, arms by his sides. I ask him if he believes his arms are truly relaxed, and of course he says yes.

I tell him to hold out his arms and hands in front of him. I then put my hands and arms under his arms, supporting them (Photo 3.37). I ask again if he believes his arms are relaxed, and he tells me, "yes."

Just as he says this, I quickly withdraw my hands and arms by pulling them down (Photo 3.38). The player's arms may lower just slightly, but they stay well up in the air (Photo 3.39). I say: "if your arms had been truly relaxed, they would have fallen to your sides."

When I say this, a light goes off in the player's head—he realizes his arms weren't relaxed.

To emphasize the point, I reverse our positions, and he sees how relaxed my arms are when he removes his arms—mine fall to my sides. We perform this exercise several times, until the player gets a feel for the relaxation we want. Perform this exercise with a friend.

Photo 3.37   Photo 3.38   Photo 3.39

The next drill is performed with a golf club. Hold a club in front of you in your normal golf grip so that the shaft is vertical (Photo 3.40).

How heavy does the club feel? Usually players say it feels very light. Now "lean" the shaft 90 degrees to one side, as in Photo 3.41—now how heavy does it feel? Much heavier.

Go back to vertical, the lightest posi-tion. Now tilt the shaft only about 45 degrees to one side, as in Photo 3.42. This is the heaviest the club should feel to you during the swing, even when it is "under speed." Close your eyes to feel this moderate pressure more vividly.

Perform this drill repeatedly to get a clear feeling of what is acceptable firm-ness in your hands and arms when you are swinging.

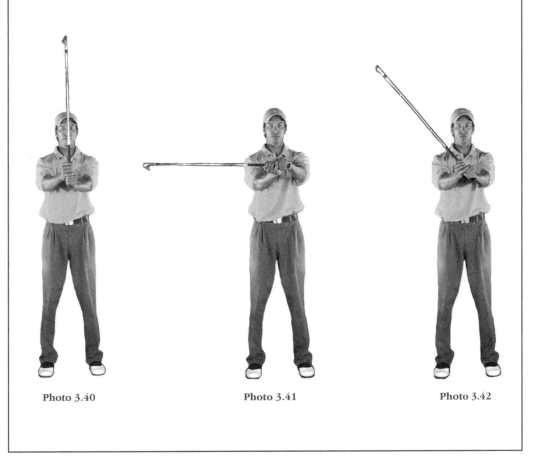

Photo 3.40   Photo 3.41   Photo 3.42

Now let's take stock a moment. Some readers, I'm sure, will feel that the order in which I'm giving these drills is arbitrary. It's not. It is an established part of my teaching, the result of much experimentation and study. The pattern here is that we build skills in order to prepare the way for the long game, while we are learning the short game. The spine angles and other postural angles, the relaxed arms and trained hands—you will work continuously on these, while you advance through putting and chipping. So by the time you take the club in your hands to hit full shots—which is some way down the road—good habits will "kick in" and the long clubs will be less intimidating, and easier.

Speaking of the long game, this is a good time to be explicit about my approach to hitting the golf ball straight, and how all the skills you are learning work into that approach.

How do you hit a ball straight? When a pro tells his student, "concentrate on direction," what does that mean? How is the student supposed to do that?

I am a very strong believer in Percy Boomer's statement that you can't hit a golf ball straight by trying to hit it straight. What you must do is understand the conditions that bring about a straight shot, and then concentrate on producing those conditions.

Our object, obviously, is to swing so the club will square up at impact. The key is to place the hands on the club in such a way, and relax the arms in such a way that when we swing the club freely the clubface will tend to true up by itself, as long as the path of the swing is correct.

This is why the proper hold of the club and relaxed arms are so important. As mentioned before, "hands equal clubface." By that I mean that once our grip and arms are conditioned, we can simply swing through freely, as if our hands were the clubface, and allow the shaft and clubhead to true up on their own.

But we can only do that if, in addition to the proper conditioning of grip and arms, we swing the club on the correct path—and that is brought about by posture and alignment.

Put it this way. The swing of the upper arms, forearms, hands, and club is a flowing motion, and it flows wherever the posture and alignment of the body allows it to flow, in the same way that the water in a rapid flows wherever the rocks allow it to flow. If we could arrange the boulders in the river, we could control where the water would flow. In a golf swing, if we can arrange where our skeleton is positioned, and how it will be aligned, we can control where the flow of the golf swing will go, and that will control the golf ball. All the skills you are learning through the skill-building exercises are designed to bring this condition about—particularly the six angles we discussed. They set the skeleton in a good position, so it can control the flow of the golf swing.

All right, that's enough lecturing for now—we go to work on the short game next, but remember to work continuously on spine angle and the other drills for the long game.

Chapter 4
Putting: Establishing the Stroke

Your work on postural angles should be continuous, even as we begin work on the short game.

Before giving you lessons in the mechanics of putting, I want to make it clear that I have a distinct philosophy and approach when it comes to the short game.

My Approach to Putting and the Short Game

The style of short game play that I teach might be called "quiet-handed" and "progressive." "Quiet-handed" means that we tone down any extra hand and wrist motion in the stroke, until we are stroking like Brad Faxon, Loren Roberts, or some of the great shoulder-arm putters of the past—Bob Charles, George Archer, or Andy North. Our stroke might not be as successful as theirs, but it's on that model.

These players used to be called "roll putters," or "shoulder putters," and they were notable for having no "pop" or "flick" in the stroke.

When we start with the "roll" putting stroke, we find that we can expand our repertoire of shots with different clubs, simply by lengthening the stroke and modifying it a bit. For chipping, the stroke will be a little more powerful, and the hands and wrists will have a little more play, but it will not feel that different from our "roll" stroke. Thus the short game strokes become progressive. We learn putts, then chip shots, then short pitch shots, with a sense of continuity in touch and mechanics.

Having a progressive short game means that when we practice one stroke, it tends to improve our performance in *all our short game strokes,* because in effect they are an extension of the same stroke.

Because our learning is progressive, our confidence builds cumulatively, and we feel self-assured, even playing difficult shots. So instead of being intimidated by such shots, we're more likely to make a good stroke with an optimistic attitude.

The only shot that I'm unable to fit into the short game progression is the bunker shot, a special shot where the club "wipes" from outside in. For that reason I generally hold off teaching bunker play until the end of a series of lessons.

If you're especially fond of another style of putting you can go back to it eventually, but during your short game lessons from me I want you to stick with the "roll" style, because we will build our other short game strokes on it.

Incidentally this type of "roll putting" didn't gain a lot of favor until the mid-1960s, when two great "roll" putters came along—Bob Charles and George Archer—who showed the world what could be achieved with this style.

The quality of the greens was also a factor. In the old days we often putted on "common" bermuda, a very coarse grass with very strong grain. Putting 40 or 50 feet uphill and upgrain required a sledgehammer blow, and the roll technique was not very good for that. But as bent became more widespread, and the high-quality hybrid bermuda strains came in, roll putting was perfect for the new "pool table" surfaces.

For me, as a teacher of "progressiveness" in the short game, it worked out beautifully, because I could modify the roll stroke for chipping, then let players get more hand and wrist into the stroke as required—for instance, handling bad lies, or greenside rough.

The Putting Grip and Setup

I always begin my putting instruction by checking very basic things such as the hold of the club, the alignment of the blade, and the proper striking on the sweet spot—it's surprising how often even good players are weak in these areas. We then go on to develop a good stroke with quiet hand motion, we learn to trust our instincts more and more, and we learn the all important drill to induce "touch." This last drill becomes the key to our whole short game.

First, the hold of the club. I recommend you choose one of these two types of grips—the most popular reverse overlap, and the "cross-handed" or "left-hand-low" hold of the club.

For the reverse overlap, instead of the club's grip passing underneath the heel of the left hand—as it's held for full shots—I recommend that the club pass up the "lifeline" of your hand (Photo 4.1). This makes the movement of your left wrist simpler during the stroke.

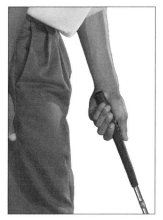

Photo 4.1   Left hand hold for a conventional reverse-overlap putting grip.

Photo 4.2   The completed reverse-overlap putting grip.

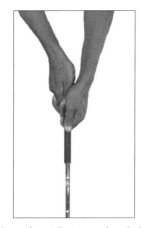

Photo 4.3   The "cross-handed" or "left-hand-low" putting grip.

Both thumbs should lie on the top of the shaft—the side directly opposite from the player—and should point straight down the shaft. When the right hand is placed on the shaft (as shown in Photo 4.2), the palms are opposite each other, the right palm parallel to the clubface. The index finger of the left hand can overlap the little finger of the right hand, or it can be more extended and overlap the little, ring, and middle finger of the right hand.

In the "left-hand-low" grip, the right hand is nearer to the player and the left hand takes the lower position on the shaft (Photo 4.3). The most important factor in using this hold of the club is that the back of the left hand be facing the target.

"Left hand low" is getting extremely popular on the PGA and LPGA tours, I think for very good reason. With this grip it's much more difficult to flick or flip with the hands, and the left hand remains in a leading position.

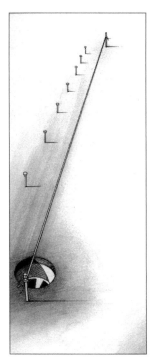

I teach putting mechanics using a "suspended string" setup, as Figure 4.1 shows. The putt chosen is preferably flat. If the green slopes at all, the putt should be straight uphill.

The string is suspended from two shafts or pegs, one of them directly behind the hole, the other down the target line, 7 to 12 feet away. Beginning players use the shorter string, experienced ones can keep performing these drills from farther out. The string passing from one shaft to the other is about 8 inches above the ground, directly over the line of the putt. Tees are placed at 1-foot intervals as markers.

Incidentally, Tiger Woods described in a magazine article how, while recovering from knee surgery in early 2003, he used a suspended string setup (very similar to the one I use, in fact) to work on his putting. And he putted beautifully in his return-to-action tournament, the Buick Invitational at Torrey Pines, which he won by four strokes.

Figure 4.1

Better Golf: A Skill Building Approach

If I'm working with a beginner I review the parts of the putter—shaft, clubhead, heel, toe and sweet spot.

So many golfers, including good ones, overlook the importance of hitting the putt on the sweet spot of the putter. For their benefit, I demonstrate by tapping the toe, then the heel of the putter, and they see how the blade deflects. Then I tap the sweet spot or center, and the blade is knocked straight back without deflecting.

I also demonstrate that if the putt is struck properly on the sweet spot, the ball travels a reliable, true distance. Struck with the same amount of force on the toe or heel, it will not get to the target.

Positive Thinking in the Short Game

Positive thinking in the short game is critical. I start right out impressing the player with the fact that putting is easy, and I want him or her to always think it's easy.

So before we even begin stroking balls, I hold up a ball and say, "the hole is 4.25 inches in diameter, and the ball is 1.68 inches in diameter. So, with this great big hole, and this tiny little ball, you should have no problem getting the ball into the hole."

You can see in the photos that two balls can roll toward the hole snugly alongside each other, and there is room for both of them to fall in. I want to firmly plant the idea in your subconscious that the hole is large, the ball is small, and the natural place for the ball to go is in the hole.

When Pia Nilsson coached the Swedish National Team in the 1990's, she told all her players to think of themselves as great putters—I believe that's one reason so many became successes on the LPGA tour. If you want to be a good putter, you must believe that you are going to be good, that the ball is likely to go in the hole, that good things will happen to you.

Test to find where you contact the clubface in putting. Spread a little talcum powder on the face of your putter before you putt. You'll be able to see immediately what your pattern is.

I want you to visualize, not a line to the hole, but a 4¼-inch lane to the hole (Photo 4.4). Think of the little stripe, about 4¼ inches wide, in the middle of the highway. Sometimes that stripe curves to the right, to the left, goes up, goes down. Visualize your lane to the hole that way—this imagery will improve your putting, much more than just visualizing a line.

Eye Alignment

On the issue of eye alignment, the old tradition in putting was that the eyes should be directly over the ball. That is, a coin dropped from the bridge of the nose would fall on the ball.

The way I teach putting alignment, a coin dropped from the bridge of the nose would fall to the right of the ball by perhaps 2 to 4 inches, as the player would look at it, but still on the target line— see Photo 4.4.

Jack Nicklaus was well known for aligning this way, but Cary Middlecoff and Jackie Burke Jr. also did, and they were both wonderful putters.

What I've discovered, over many years of teaching putting, is that *by far the majority of players performs better with the Nicklaus alignment* than they do with the "bridge of the nose over the ball" alignment.

So when I start off, I give players the option of both alignments, but I make it clear that the majority do better with their eyes back of the ball. Then they decide.

Photo 4.4   Eyes behind the ball, visualizing the lane to the hole.

As for relationship to the target line, I prefer that the player align so that a coin dropped from the bridge of the nose would land on the target line. It's true that some players are successful aligning so that the coin would land on the same side of the target line that the player is standing on—Justin Leonard is a good example. If the player has a strong preference that way, I'll allow that. I never allow my students to get the eyes out beyond the line—no one has ever succeeded with that alignment.

The Stroke

Once we have gone over the hold of the club, and eye alignment, put aside your club and rehearse your putting stroke only with your hands—which makes the feeling of the proper stroke easier to identify. Do this either with your hands in "prayer" position, or with the slight "set" of the hands and wrists that I teach on the next page.

When we are putting, we don't need to use this "set," but I like players to practice and learn it early on, because as the shots become more powerful, it becomes more essential.

Work with your "string setup" to establish your stroke.

First, stand in a comfortable putting stance, hands in "prayer" position, and lowered to approximately the position they would occupy holding a club. When you close your right eye and look down out of your left eye, your thumbnails should be aligned directly on your line of sight to the string, as you see in Figure 4.2. Stroke back and forth, your thumbnails staying on the target line for several inches in either direction before they move "inside" the string. The figure indicates this back and forth motion.

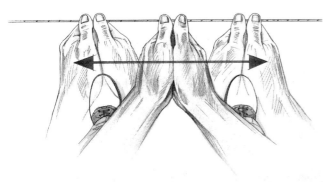

Figure 4.2

The "tray" drill is a traditional drill to learn the set of the hands and wrists for the power clubs, although many of my students find it helpful for putting and the short game, as well. Set the right hand as if you were a waiter holding a tray, but with the palm at 45 degrees to horizontal, not 90 as a waiter would hold it (Photo 4.5). Then put the left hand on with the back of the left hand in line with the left forearm (Photo 4.6). Then lower the arms down into an address position (Photos 4.7, 4.8). You can see the slight curve between the back of the right hand and the right forearm. That "set" remains during the stroke, but make sure the "set" is soft—you do not stiffen the wrist.

Photo 4.5

Photo 4.6

Photo 4.7

Photo 4.8

Physically a putting stroke can never be like a pendulum, but I want you to give this stroke the *rhythm* of a pendulum.

Stroke back and forth with the triangle of your shoulders and arms several times (Photo 4.9), until you get into a rhythm. Then, as you are stroking, picture me reaching out with both hands and holding your head still as you stroke (Photo 4.10). And if at all possible get a spouse or friend to actually take hold of your head in this fashion. This simple action causes a great release of tension—many players comment on this. It "oils" their shoulders, so they move freely without the head moving.

Many players are like the Tin Man in The Wizard of Oz, when he is in need of oil. Tight shoulders are the surest sign of tension in a golfer. If the player really is having trouble, I will sometimes make the stroke for him, holding his head in one hand and his hands in the other, as you see in Photo 4.11.

Photo 4.9   Photo 4.10

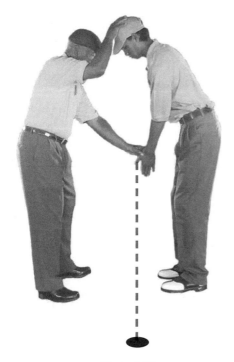

Photo 4.11

As you stroke, keep your thumbs "on the line" as in Figure 4.2. We want the body motionless except for the arms and shoulders—so check for any swaying, jiggling, or body action with a partner or a mirror.

While I hold a player's head still, I even say in timing with the stroke, "tick, tock, like a clock." I want to induce a very quiet frame of mind in players, an almost meditative state, where they are not aware of success or failure or nervousness or fear, and are only aware of the feeling they are seeking.

Incidentally it's much easier to achieve this quiet state of mind without a golf club, without a golf ball, and without wondering what sort of putt we're going to produce. All those things excite the mind and distract it from learning the "feel" we desire.

When the thumbs have moved back a few inches in a player's backswing, they start to move inside the line—you shouldn't worry about that or try to prevent it. The same thing happens forward of the ball. There is a space of about 5 or 6 inches where the thumbs are approximately on the line. Eventually you will get to the point where you can make a stroke *without a club and with your eyes closed,* and you will be able to tell whether that stroke would have holed the putt, or missed it.

Our next steps are to work with the "hanger drill" for a better stroke (next page), then adjust weight distribution.

On the subject of weight distribution, at this point, put 60% of your weight on your left side, but without leaning like the Tower of Pisa. Then continue to stroke with your hands in prayer position. You will see that, with the weight on the left side, the thumbnails stay

The "hanger drill" reinforces the feeling of the roll stroke. Players are always delighted with how much feel they get for the stroke this way, and the hands become very quiet.

Insert your arms through a coat hanger, and simply stroke back and forth with no club but with the hands in a prayer position (photos 4.12 and 4.13).

Please realize that I am not promoting "stiff-wristed" putting. The hands and wrists should never be stiff, they should always be fluid and easy in their movement. But the shoulders and arms should be controlling the stroke, with the hands and wrists remaining pliable.

Photo 4.12

Photo 4.13

"on the line" a little longer in the forward swing. The weight on the left also stabilizes the body, which is an advantage. Usually players agree to that adjustment, weight 60-40 on the left. If the player prefers 50-50, I let him or her stay there.

Now we are ready to take the putter in our hands and perform the five essential drills to establish putting mechanics. Each of these has a purpose.

Five Drills for Putting Mechanics

The following five drills give you a good grounding in putting mechanics, and they are a very good diagnostic and correction tool as well.

If I am working with a novice golfer, or a player having trouble with putting, I ask him or her to perform each of these five drills every day for a week. For more experienced players, the five drills are a fallback in times of trouble—many players have told me that a review of these drills pulled them out of a slump.

The one-armed drill makes your stroke more solid and assured.

You will hole three balls from 1 foot out, holding the putter in your left hand only (Photo 4.14). Then you hole three balls with the putter in only your right hand (Photo 4.15). Repeat from two feet, three feet, and if you can from 4 feet. If you miss, you can have one retry, but that's all, or you'll lose your rhythm.

If one of your hands/arms is not doing its job, the deficiency becomes clear, and you should *practice short putts holding the club in that hand alone* until proficient.

Photo 4.14   Photo 4.15

In my first putting lesson with each pupil, the five drills are performed using the string setup on page 60. After that, the pupil performs without the string, unless he or she is working on alignment.

The push drill gets to the core of my short game teaching, because it helps the player to "roll" the ball, rather than flick at it. We use the three balls and start with the 1 foot putt. Set the clubface against the ball in a normal address position, clubface properly aligned (Photo 4.16). *Without a backswing,* and keeping the head steady, simply *push* the putt into the hole (Photo 4.17). The task is to hole out three times from 1 foot, from 2 feet, all the way to 5 feet. Don't worry over missed putts, but keep going and keep your performance rhythmic.

Players who have a flick or "pop" in the stroke—some even have a "jab-and-recoil" action—find that this drill quiets down the hand motion, and they get a steady forward flowing motion of the clubhead through the ball. This quieting of the hands is extremely valuable for "touch" and scoring, and the result is worth a great deal of time spent.

Photo 4.16   Photo 4.17

With the basketball drill we start to transfer the trust to the subconscious, which we must do in putting, as in full shots. Before I introduce the drill, let's get a little feeling of trusting the subconscious. Put down your club. Now, close your eyes, put your forefingers in front of you, and bring them together with your eyes closed.

Sometimes players have trouble which is due to tension, and I remind them to relax. Then they do it easily.

Next do the same thing, but touching your forefingers together *behind you*. Once relaxed, you'll find that you are able to do that easily as well.

Isn't the body a wonderful machine? That exercise should tell you—the subconcious always knows where the hands are, what they're doing. The computer inside the body can do wonderful things, if we just relax, and let it go.

Try this exercise again—it wlll put you in a good frame of mind for transferring trust to your subconscious.

We now perform the basketball drill, so called because you look at the target while stroking, like a basketball player looking at the basket.

Again, we use three balls and start with 1 foot putts. Once you have addressed the ball normally, *look at the hole* and stroke the putt.

When players putt in this way, and succeed, they become surprised, excited. Some even ask me if they can putt that way on the golf course. I say, "why not?"

The drill is holing three balls from 1 foot, from 2 feet, from 3 feet, and, for advanced players, 4 feet.

You will learn that even when you get back to looking at the ball, you have a subliminal sense of the target, which will guide your actions. You don't need to putt this way on the course, but this gives you the message to trust your subconscious.

The next drill is to strike putts looking at the front edge of the ball, the part nearest the hole. We engage in the same progression, starting with three balls from a foot out, ending with three balls from 4 feet out.

This helps you keep the putter on line longer, keep it accelerating through the ball, and this drill helps you hold your head in place and your shoulders in plane until the ball is well away. This is important. Even on the touring level, you often see putting strokes where the head comes up and the shoulders open to the hole prematurely, leading to a pulled putt.

It's also helpful to *hold the finish* of the putting stroke—it helps keep the shoulders square and the head still, and later it will help to gauge distance with longer putts.

By this point you are getting enough feel for your stroke that, with the proper drilling, you can sense whether or not a putt has been successful *without the putter, and with your eyes closed.*

So let's perform the drill without a putter, which is a step toward the blindfold drill.

Set yourself up to the suspended string, and put your hands down in the prayer position so that your thumbs are "right on the string" as you look out of your left eye. Then close your eyes and stroke back and forth as if to hit a 6-foot putt, hold your finish, and open your eyes. If your thumbs are "right on the string," you would have holed the putt. If they are out beyond the string, your stroke would have pushed the putt. If they are on your side of the string, you would have pulled the putt.

This is not an abstract idea, it really works. Enough of this practice, and you get the feel of a good stroke into your system. You also learn to trust this stroke, and stop adding the little flips and flickings that you may have had in the past.

After giving yourself this "stroke test," move on to the blindfold drill.

The procedure is to address the ball, close your eyes, and stroke the ball into the hole. Again we start by putting three balls from 1 foot out, and increase the distance by a foot every three balls.

After a certain point of working with these drills, you will feel that you have developed a sound stroke. After that, don't think about mechanics, just let the stroke flow, visualize the ball traveling along the 4¼-inch lane and going into the hole. Trust your subconscious to get the ball to the target.

Dispense with the string, after the first lesson. The string is extremely helpful with beginners and those who want to work on their alignment—as Tiger Woods did while recovering from his knee surgery. But I don't want players to keep setting the string up for each practice session, or it will become a crutch.

Practicing Touch

Good mechanics are fine, but they are not what makes a great putter. What makes a great putter is the ability to *feel the ball into the hole*—which comes from *touch*.

We gain touch through what I call the ladder drill (next page)—the key drill of the entire short game. I have found this drill to be the most effective drill of all for improving scoring.

I could give literally a hundred examples of the effectiveness of the ladder drill—here is one:

In the late 1990's I was teaching at the Willow Glen Golf Course at Great Lakes Naval Training Center, north of Chicago, and I gave putting lessons to a retired naval instructor who had already become a friend of mine, Charles Overstreet. Charles was a former low-handicap player who had just returned from a long, golf-less tour of duty. His long game got in shape quickly, but putting was holding him back. He was averaging about 36 putts a round.

I sent him through the mechanical drills, and his mechanics were fine. So we set up for the ladder drill. His first putt stopped 18 inches short of the first tee. His second rolled 3 feet past the second tee. We had found our problem.

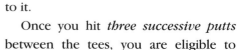

This drill requires three tees and three balls. You can perform the drill indoors on a rug, standing the tees upside down.

Put one tee in the ground as a marker—from beside this tee, the balls will be struck. Place a target tee 12 feet away, and another tee 18 inches beyond the target tee, on the same line (Figure 4.3).

You will hit three putts, and the object is to roll the ball past the first tee, but not past the second tee. The exact line is not really relevant here—pay no attention to it.

Once you hit *three successive putts* between the tees, you are eligible to move back to 14 feet. Three successes in a row, and you can move to 16 feet, which is the longest distance I give players when they start with this drill. (If you happen to be an exceptional putter, you can eventually move back to 18 or even 20 feet.)

I call this the *ladder drill,* because when you succeed three times in a row, you advance to another rung. Over a playing and teaching career spanning 50 years, I have found this to be *by far the best of all drills for the entire short game,* not just for putting.

Figure 4.3

He practiced the ladder drill almost every day. Less than a month later, Charles won the club championship, using 26 putts for his round and holing a 25-foot putt on the final green. The ladder drill alone brought his scores from 79–82 down to 73–76.

Charles, of course, was a very good player. But this drill is even more helpful for middle- and upper-handicappers. Ladder practice means that they'll get better touch on the putting green, but also with their other shots. When they face a 60-foot chip with a 7-iron, for instance, they're likely to leave the ball 5 feet away, instead of 15 feet away. More and more often they "roll three shots into two," and their scores improve dramatically.

I tell all players that they should practice the ladder drill *daily*, if they have the opportunity, indoors or outdoors. *The ladder drill, and continuing work on their body angles, become the keys to maintaining their games.*

If you practice this drill on various greens where you play, and you travel for golf, you learn how to deal with grasses in different sections of the country—how fast greens are in different seasons, how tightly the greens have been mowed that day, how brown or green they are, whether the grass is sparse or thick, etc. These factors are constantly changing. If you perform this drill before each round, over the course of six months the difference in your ability to read greens will be amazing.

The ladder drill is also the best form of warming up. If your time before teeing off is limited, perform some stretches, perform the ladder drill, and you'll be better off than if you hit balls.

One thing to keep in mind: don't try to succeed at the ladder drill by some mechanical contrivance, such as "so many inches of backswing for how many feet the putt is long." Once you are sound mechanically, learning touch must be left up to your instinct—don't become too mechanical.

I've advised you to practice the ladder drill—using three balls—before each round. However, as you wind up your pre-round putting practice, always finish up with some meticulous practice using one ball.

Go through the putting clock on the practice green with that ball, treating each hole exactly as you would on the golf course, down to marking your ball and brushing off impediments in your line. This helps to sharpen your focus in your final preparation, because on the golf course you will get only one chance.

On the matter of how short or long the putting stroke should be, I've found that it doesn't matter—it's a case of individual preference. I simply tell the players to work at the ladder drill, and whatever length of stroke they come to, that will work.

Golfers who hit short shots *at* the hole are never great scorers. Once you get a sense of distance, and start hitting the ball with touch and feel, lagging it *to* the hole with all your clubs, you're on your way to much lower scores.

Chapter 5
Chipping and Short Pitching

Bobby Jones once wrote, "all good golfers are great chippers." I agree. Chipping is crucial in my scheme of teaching, first because it's such a great stroke saver, and second because it's a key transition in our progression from putter to shotmaker.

I'm extremely successful at turning players into good chippers, even if they come to me saying they "can't chip." Before the 45 minutes is up, the players have usually holed out several times and come away with a different attitude, and a different chipping game.

The key to this success is that I separate the elements of good chipping, and teach them *in steps,* as I will explain. This chapter is written so that the reader can work on his chipping on a practice green, or even indoors on the rug, if that would be more convenient.

Now, about my three-step program: The steps are: (1) chipping with a square stance and the ball played off the right foot, until the feeling of the shoulders being square is firmly implanted in the subconscious—in a 45-minute lesson this takes the first 20 minutes; (2) adopting an open stance with the ball played more toward the middle of the stance, but still with square shoulders; and (3) staying with the second stance, but engaging the legs in the stroke, using a so-called "rocking chair" motion like the one used by Tom Watson or Byron Nelson.

We'll follow that sequence in this chapter, except that between the second and third steps, I've added drills to reinforce what we're learning.

Some of these drills involve props, but these are easily found at home—the frame of a door and an old pillow to serve as an impact bag.

Let's start out, then, hitting chip shots from our initial setup with a 7- or 8-iron. If we are outdoors, the patch of green we choose should be level or going slightly uphill away from us, the hole about 25 feet away. If you are indoors, the target can be a tumbler or a tee upside down.

It's important for your chipping that you have already worked a good deal on your posture at this point.

As in putting, you will address with square shoulders and stroke with "quiet" hands. But there are adjustments. We change from the reverse overlap to the overlapping grip. We adjust the stroke to produce a more *descending* blow. We make sure our weight *starts left, stays left* during the backswing, and *moves even more left during the forward stroke.*

Once we get these factors in line and work on our stroke, I find that players "fill up the cup" with their chip shots.

Chip from Setup #1

Our first step is to chip for 10 to 20 minutes from address setup #1, as shown in Figure 5.1. The stance is square. The ball is played off the right instep. The shoulders are in plane with the target line, as with putting. The weight favors the left leg by about 60%-40%.

We place a second ball 12 inches opposite the target from the ball to be struck. You must swing the clubhead back so that it will clear the second ball, which trains you to make a descending blow.

Stand as close to the ball as you can without crowding yourself. It is almost impossible to stand too close to the ball when chipping.

Two things to be sure of as you chip are that (1) your weight

Figure 5.1
Chipping setup #1.

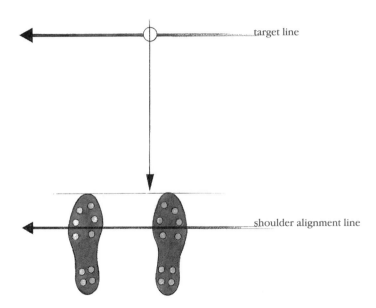

starts to the left and stays to the left, and (2) the clubhead always lags behind your hands until the ball is struck.

We've spoken before about the tendency of the golfer to "flick" forward with his dominant hand. Because this impulse causes such damage, I demonstrate it as shown in Photo 5.1, without a club, and with the hands in the prayer position. This photo shows what happens when the right arm straightens, *or* the right wrist straightens. It's evident how the left wrist *collapses*—if we are holding a club, the butt of the club "backs up" during the stroke.

The weight should remain on the left side as we swing back, and it moves targetward as we swing through.

The hands and wrists remain loose and pliable, but the hands never dominate the motion.

Later, when we learn shots for special conditions, we will allow more hand and wrist motion—for instance when we're getting the ball out of greenside rough. But these specialty shots are learned later.

Photo 5.1

| Photo 5.2 | Photo 5.3 | Photo 5.4 |

Practicing chip shots with an extra ball 12 inches back of the object ball trains the player to make a crisp descending blow.

Pause to Check Alignment—After you have chipped from setup #1 for 20 minutes or so, move around the practice green if you are outside, toss down balls in several locations, and address each in turn as if you are chipping to the flag. Once your position at the ball is settled, freeze your body and legs where they are, place the club across your chest, and see whether your torso and shoulders are aligned in plane with the target line. This drill is needed, because the quieter the hands in the short game, the more important shoulder alignment becomes.

80

Chip from Setup #2

Next we move on to setup #2—the one you will ultimately use in play.

We open up the feet—the stance is more open *and* the toes are pointed more toward the target, as Figure 5.2 shows. The feet should be angled 15 degrees to 20 degrees to the left of straight. We also move the ball position to the center of the stance.

However, *the shoulders stay in plane with the target line.* This is a "make or break" point in chipping.

Standing to a chip with my feet and shoulders *open,* I can demonstrate that, although you can hit good chips from here, the natural tendency is to pull from this position.

Then I show a position of open stance but square shoulders. This gives the player a lot of advantages: Better sight down the line, better body motion through contact, and freer passage for the right hand to move toward the target during the stroke.

You now have the option of staying with setup #1 if you prefer—most players adopt setup #2. Chip for 15 or 20 minutes from the new setup and make sure that the combination of square shoulders and open stance has become comfortable.

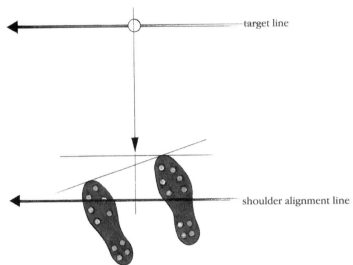

target line

shoulder alignment line

Figure 5.2
Chipping setup #2.

Five Checkup Drills

The following are checkup drills to re-affirm what you're learning, or to help if you are having persistent trouble. And players can tell when they're having persistent trouble with their chipping, because there's plenty of miserable feedback—they skull the ball or hit the ground behind it, hit chips way past the hole, and so on.

SKILL BUILDER *Impact Bag Drill*

This drill involves an impact bag—if you don't have one, simply use an old pillow, or fill a pillowcase with old clothes and tie the end off—that will work fine.

Place the impact bag where the ball would normally be, get into chipping address #2 (Photo 5.7), then move your hands toward the imaginary target until you get resistance from the bag (Photo 5.8)—notice how you are not breaking your wrists—the clubhead is not moving ahead of your hands. You can feel the "set" your hands and wrists get in—then make a little backswing (Photo 5.9) and forward swing into the bag, very gently (Photo 5.10). If you have trouble "flipping," perform this drill over and over again, even 1000 times, until you get to the point where the wrists do not break.

Photo 5.7

Photo 5.8

Photo 5.9

Photo 5.10

Better Golf: A Skill Building Approach

Address a dry sponge or other cushioning object placed in the corner of a door jamb as indicated in Photo 5.11. Draw back the clubhead and strike the sponge a very easy blow, only hard enough to hit a 7 iron chip 10 or 15 feet. When the clubhead comes against the sponge, keep it pressed there, don't let it rebound away. It's an easy stroke, but ending with the clubhead frozen against the sponge. Work with the drill until your hands don't break down going through the chipping stroke.

Photo 5.11

Photo 5.12

Hit chips holding the club in only the right hand, then only the left hand. This is great training for all short game shots, because it shores up the stroke, and reveals weaknesses clearly. If you perform badly holding the club in one hand, practice with the club in only that hand until you're more assured with it.

This drill can be performed with a club or simply with your hands in the prayer position. Stand in an address position with your left hip leaned against the frame of a doorway, stabilized on your left side. Swing the triangle of your shoulders and arms back and through. A good deal of this drilling will teach you to *stay on your left side.*

In this drill, you will practice chips standing on the flat of the left foot, but only the toe of the right foot, with the right foot withdrawn from the target line about 10 inches—see Photo 5.13. This stabilizes you on your left side, because you can't shift your weight, or you will fall over.

Photo 5.13

I got a lesson in the value of quiet hands back around 1960, when I was at the peak of my game.

I was playing frequently at the Butler course near McKeesport, Pennsylvania, where my friend Johnny Waters played—he was a mid-70s shooter who had introduced me to golf.

I was in the clubhouse one day when Jimmy Nichols came to play. Jimmy was a pro who had lost his right arm in an accident. He played holding the club in only his left hand, swinging backhanded. He had become such a good player he was under contract to an equipment company, and he would tour through an area, play the local course, and give a clinic.

I was a pretty good player, shooting around par, and was asked to play Jimmy. On the first tee he wanted to have a friendly wager on the side, playing for dinner. I thought this would be the easiest meal I ever earned.

Jimmy shot 71, playing beautiful golf. I made quite a number of mistakes and shot 78. I didn't get flustered, but I certainly was stunned by his skill. He hit the ball as long as I did, which was 240 to 250 yards, the equivalent of 270 with today's equipment. And he had great touch in the short game.

After the round I was prepared to buy Jimmy an expensive dinner. He could have had anything on the menu. He ordered boiled eggs and beer. That happened to be his favorite combination. And we had a wonderful conversation about great players he had played with, adjustments he had made as a one-armed player, and so on.

What made Jimmy's short game so great was that he never had to worry about the forward flick of the right hand—there was no right hand. He stroked with a smooth pace through the short game shots, and developed great touch.

This shows you why quieting that forward flicking movement is so important. Quiet the hands, stroke with your triangle, perform the ladder drill a good deal, and you will start to feel the difference between, for instance, a 22-foot chip and a 30-foot chip. More and more you will develop your sense of touch, and that is the greatest scoring weapon in golf—once you've hit the fairway.

I tell players: "if you can control your distance, you'll be a match for anyone that you play."

Rocking Chair Leg Motion

Once we've gone through these drills, we're ready to perfect the leg action of the stroke. I tell my students to visualize Tom Watson hitting a chip, because his chip and short pitch swing is my ideal—the perfect blend of movement of the triangle and the legs.

To learn this action yourself, follow this sequence: Address the chip shot with address #2. Swing the triangle (of arms and shoulders) back (Photo 5.14), then forward (Photo 5.15)—and as you swing it forward, feel the right knee going forward at the same time, just as Watson does it. You don't force the knee to move, it should naturally get in motion, but be aware of it.

Some players will even feel that they "make the shot with the knees," the left knee moving a little at the target also, and that's fine. This is the "rocking chair" motion in short pitching, practiced by great players like Watson and Byron Nelson. Notice that as the legs

Photo 5.14

Photo 5.15

become more active, the hands are less inclined to flip or flick. You'll notice also with this rocking chair motion that you get a crisp, clean contact and a lot of spin on the ball. You'll become bolder and more confident with all short wedge shots.

Please note that, for the sake of the proper order of learning, it's not a wise idea to introduce this "knee movement" earlier in the sequence of learning chipping, because you get too many details to absorb and become confused. It's better to introduce it only after working extensively with setup #1, setup #2, and the five drills.

Your next step is to start striking longer wedge shots—from 20 yards up to 50 yards. Don't try to do anything special with these shots, strike them as an extension of your chipping stroke. You should feel, simply from the momentum of the stroke, that your hands and wrists will "break" more between backswing and forward swing—just let that happen naturally. Also, as the shot gets longer, work on developing an adhesion of the upper left arm to the ribcage, and even practice with a golf glove or club head cover under the left arm. This adhesion helps unite the arm swing and body action and will become more important as the shots get longer.

Learning Variety and Creativity

Once you have worked to develop your stroke, I want you to develop variety in your chipping game and *use a variety of clubs.* Some golfers develop a "pet" chipping club—often a sand wedge—which they use regardless of the situation. I don't think that's a good idea. There are too many different situations that come up, and you must be equipped to handle them.

You might be on the front fringe of a double-tiered green 50 yards long, with the flag at the back. If you chip with your pet sand wedge, you will rarely get the ball back near the hole; whereas if you hit a firm low shot with a 5-iron, you're likely to do much better. Dif-

Aggressiveness in the Short Game

As you get better and better with your short game, a psychological change takes place. When you miss a green, you don't feel a letdown. Instead, you feel a sense of optimism, because you have a chance to show what a great short game player you are.

That mental attitude was so characteristic of players like Raymond Floyd, Kathy Whitworth, Tom Watson, and Seve Ballesteros. When they missed a green and had a short shot to play, they seemed to relish the situation. And their opponents couldn't relax, because these players might hole out from anywhere. Don't think, "I missed the green," think, "Wait until you see this chip."

ferent situations demand different clubs. And in all cases, you want the ball to roll more than it flies, if possible.

So develop variety, and remember that all along you should practice the ladder drill with your putter, and even with your chipping clubs, which develops the touch you need to hit all these shots close to the hole.

We are now ready for our "leap" to the long game. But we don't accomplish this by simply starting to hit longer shots. As I've said, the most effective way to advance in golf is to learn putting, chipping, short pitches up to about 50 yards, and *don't* go farther than that. Instead, take the golf ball and club out of the picture altogether, dismantle the habits of a good full shot ballstriker, and teach those habits to your subconscious one by one, through drilling.

Of course, pupils want to hit golf balls. But once they have their first successes doing my drills, they become convinced.

Chapter 6
Ball Position and Alignment

In the game of most golfers, the "leap to full swings" is a disappointing one. They arrive at the golf course or practice range full of high hopes, and many miscues later, they go home disgusted and ready to quit.

My method of producing success in the student's long game is to teach the short game while preparing the player for the long game, in terms of not only posture—which we have already learned—but in terms of the body alignment at address and body motion during the swing—which we are about to learn.

It is always necessary to hit balls in order to get better. But with a maximum of preparation in these areas, we undergo the least amount of disappointment and frustration in developing our long game.

The next three chapters, then, are on ball position and alignment, the pivot, and blending the pivot with the arm movement.

In addition, throughout these chapters, I have inserted sidebars on "becoming a shot maker." These learning hints apply to all shots, from chips all the way to drives, and it will be good for your game if you read and reread them, as you work on your preparation for the long game. You will notice that almost all of these pointers pertain to target orientation, and relaxation and balance of the body. Those are vitally important, so work on them, even as you work on your alignment and pivot.

Ball Position and Alignment

I am more than a stickler for exact ball position and alignment because my own game improved by about eight shots in eighteen months due largely to improvements in that area. This occurred in the late 1950's, when I was being taught by Richard Grout, the brother of Jack Nicklaus's teacher, Jack Grout. I got down to scratch in 18 months of hard work, and I've been able to do for others what Grout did for me.

Keep Posture Upright and Look at the Target More Than the Ball

Every player at address looks back and forth from the target to the ball. Make sure that you glance at the ball only briefly, and spend a much longer time looking at the target. And keep your posture upright, with your chin well up (Photo 6.1).

Watch good players, and you'll see they do these two things. Watch high handicappers, and you'll see that they often bend over and become fixated with the ball, as if counting the dimples on it, and hardly look at the target at all. We professionals call this "ball bound," and it is the sign of a high handicapper. Instead stay tall, and look at the target more than the ball.

Photo 6.1

This lesson is one of my most demanding—certainly no other teacher I've seen goes into the detail that I do. But it's for a reason.

Most golfers go through their lives with *approximate* ball position and *approximate* alignment, and they never realize that *these things can be made very exacting*—and the more exacting they are made, the better it is for the player.

When playing golf we should not be like the hockey player hitting a slap shot—getting the ball in approximate position and then swiping at it, counting on our eye-hand coordination to make the shot successful. We should be as exact as humanly possible.

Understand Tension and How to Combat It

Most golfers become tense without knowing it, much less knowing what to do about it.

When tension creeps in, two things happen—the hands tighten their grip, and the shoulders "bunch up," as if the player is trying to touch them to his ears—particularly the right shoulder (Photo 6.2).

Make sure that you maintain an easy hold of the club, largely in your fingers. In lessons I encourage the player to hold the club gently, as though it were something delicate. Sam Snead used to say you should hold the club as if it were a captive bird—you didn't want it to get away, but you didn't want to hurt it.

If you sense that your shoulders are bunching up, imagine that you had heavy but soft weights, one on each shoulder, pressing your shoulders gently down into a more relaxed position, almost droop-shouldered. Take a long, deep breath. Then swing the club.

Photo 6.2

Your goals from this lesson in ball position and alignment are these:

- You address the ball with a given club so that the relative positions of your body, hands, clubshaft, clubhead and ball are consistent within a quarter of an inch (or less) each time.

- You address with the clubface properly pointing at the target.

- You address with the manufacturer's loft on the club—that is, with the sole or bottom of the club flat to the ground, as it was designed to be soled.

- The distance from the butt of the club to your body is consistent for iron shots (about 4 inches).

- The whole address procedure is a steady routine, repeating with consistency.

Altogether, this is quite an assignment, but the improvement for your game is worth it.

Focus on Target, Not Mechanics

In this book I give you drills to use, to teach mechanics to your subconscious. After that is done, golf becomes a target game. You already know how to hold the club and address the ball and align yourself. Now just get the ball to the target. If you get over a ball at address thinking "what do I do first, what do I do second, . . ." you haven't trained enough. More drilling is needed.

Exercise Depth Perception

Exercise your depth perception and develop the ability to judge distance. If the marker says it's 150 yards, look at the shot. Does it *look* like 150 yards? Is it uphill? Is the wind against you? Ask yourself, "do I feel comfortable hitting this club?" Don't just "play by the numbers." Factor the numbers in, certainly, but play by feel.

Figure 6.1 Loft angle   Figure 6.2 Lie angle

This lesson can be learned indoors or out. You need three clubs and a ball, and if you are indoors a mirror will be helpful.

The first thing I do when I teach this lesson in person is demonstrate the importance of a square clubface. I hit three chip shots, first with an open face, next with a closed face, and last with a square face—the first ball goes right, the second left, and the third straight.

Believe it or not, this simple exercise strikes a chord with many of my students, even those who are skilled players. It had never struck them so forcefully how much the clubface position influences the direction of the shot.

The club has both a loft angle and a lie angle (see Figures 6.1 and 6.2). The loft angle is simply the wedging effect built into the club. This allows the player to swing as if to strike the ball straight forward along the gound, allowing the club to create the flight. The lie angle is the angle between the sole of the club and the clubshaft. These factors seem elementary, but you must be aware of them.

What have you been taught about ball position? If you are like most of my pupils your answer is that, as the loft of the club increases, the ball is played more and more toward the right foot.

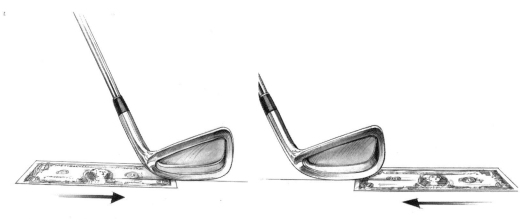

Figure 6.3a   Figure 6.3b

In my teaching we change this. My pupils are taught to address the ball 3 to 4 inches inside the left heel for every normal flat lie, but in each case to put the maker's loft on the club. This applies to every club except the driver, which is a special case, as I will explain.

To explain the maker's loft, take several clubs by the head, and lay each club down on its sole, on a raised surface near eye level, so you can observe closely. You are trying to get the clubhead to sit as flat on its sole as possible. Run a dollar bill under the clubhead from the heel side and toe side (Photos 6.3a, 6.3b). Make sure the club is not leaning onto the front edge of its sole, or back onto the back edge of its sole.

The clubhead is now sitting as the club maker designed it to sit. Addressing the ball with the maker's loft on the club, and with the face pointing directly at the target, makes it much easier to swing in the proper plane, and get a crisp strike.

But there's a further point to be made, which will influence our address. To show this to the student, I hold the head of a long iron up at eye level, with the maker's loft on the club, and ask the student to stand out from the toe of the club and see how the shaft is angled.

I was first taught ball position and alignment games by Richard Grout, the brother of Jack Grout, who taught Jack Nicklaus. The Grout brothers were sticklers for getting these details exact. Practicing them made my shotmaking improve.

The most notable change was how much more accurately I began hitting irons. Previously a good 8-iron shot might end up 15 or 18 feet from the hole. Now it was more like 8 or 10 feet. I was constantly giving myself birdie opportunities, which made a great difference in my scoring—as it will in yours.

Then I do the same with a more lofted club—and the student sees that the shafts are angled differently.

The shafts of the long irons are angled so that, when the sole of the club is flat on the ground, the butt of the club is about even with the ball. The shafts of the more lofted clubs (6-iron through the wedges) are angled more toward the target, so the butt of the club is ahead of the clubface. We will get back to this point later, but I want you to be aware of it right away.

It's also essential, when you begin this lesson, that you've done a good deal of preparatory work on your spine angle, so that angle will be virtually the same, every time you step up to the ball.

If you haven't done your spine angle work, don't confuse yourself by studying this chapter prematurely. Perform the work on your spine angle from chapter three, then take this lesson.

The initial skill of laying the club down accurately so its face is perpendicular to the target line is crucial. When I'm teaching in person I can see what a player is doing, but for those reading this book it's important to be able to self-check this point.

Checking Clubface Alignment

Find a room in your house that has a tile floor, with square tiles. Stand at one end of the room, and address an imaginary ball at a perpendicular intersection of two lines. At the other end of the room you can see where the "target line" goes (Figure 6.4)—address an imagi-

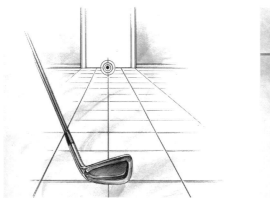

Figure 6.4 Checking clubface alignment

Figure 6.5 Properly square

nary shot at that target. Then check how the leading edge of the club snugs up to the line perpendicular to the target line. You'll discover that your pattern is consistent—you tend to align the clubface either slightly closed, or slightly open, or properly square (Figure 6.5). If you align it habitually closed or open, practice this exercise a good deal until you can set the club properly.

Incidentally, if you tend to slice, and you see by the above test that you tend to address with the clubface closed, the transition to a square face will be awkward at first. The clubface will look open at address, and then, when you hit several shots to the right—as you will starting

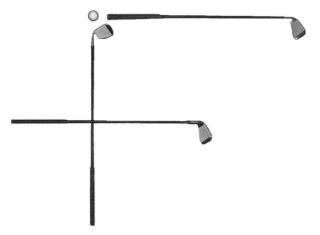

off—you will begin to wonder about the wisdom of my advice. Be patient, and stick with it. In a little time, you will become comfortable with a square face.

For the standard lesson in ball position, the player puts down three clubs and a ball as shown in Photo 6.3, one club representing the target line, one representing the shoul-

Photo 6.3 Three clubs and a ball from player's view at address. Top club shows target line, middle club shows shoulder line.

Better Golf: A Skill Building Approach

der and hip alignment, and one passing from the ball toward the player, perpendicular to the other two.

I want all players to develop a repeating routine in approaching the ball, like the routine a basketball player repeats before a free throw. This relaxes the player and prevents too many conscious thoughts, which aren't helping at that point.

In the routine that I recommend, you start from directly *behind* the ball, facing the target, holding the club (Photo 6.4). You then walk up beside the ball, and from a position fairly near it, with your right foot nearest it, put the clubhead behind the ball, flat on its sole, and facing the target, with the leading edge of the club perpendicular to the target line (Photo 6.5). Then place your left foot 3 to 4 inches to the target side of a position even with the ball (Photo 6.6).

Next step out with your right foot, spreading the stance to the proper width (Photo 6.7). The sequence and the rhythm of this procedure should be very consistent from shot to shot.

Your width of stance will depend on your build and flexibility. As a rule, too wide a stance will restrict the turn, and too narrow a

Photo 6.4   Photo 6.5   Photo 6.6   Photo 6.7

stance will cause you to lose your balance during the swing. I allow some leeway here to find out what works best for you.

It is also important to regulate the distance from the butt of the club to the body at address. To check it, take your normal grip and address, then take the right hand off the club and use the breadth of your hand to check this distance. Then re-attach the right hand. For all iron clubs the distance from the butt of the club to the body should be about 4 inches. For fairway woods and the driver, the distance is closer to 6 inches.

Also there's the question of which way the feet should be pointed. Ben Hogan said that we should place the right foot perpendicular to the line, the left foot toed out a quarter turn. And that has become the standard in teaching the stance. It's not a bad rule of thumb, but I think there must be room for adjustment—most importantly, your stance should not conflict with your natural walking gait.

If I teach a player who is a little bowlegged and has a left foot turned in, I don't fight that too much. Such a player will usually play his best golf with the left foot perpendicular to the line, or slightly toed in, and with no attempt to incline the knees toward each other. If you walk with your feet toed out, it's likely that you'll play your best golf with them toed out.

If you are a senior, particularly if you're having trouble getting distance, consider one of two changes—either withdrawing the right foot from the line a bit—using a slightly more closed stance—or pointing the right foot a little more to the right. Some seniors will need to make both those adjustments. Experiment with them—you might gain 10–15 yards in a hurry.

Address for Power Clubs

Now we come to a critical point: how to control the positioning of the ball, club, and hands relative to each other, so they will stay in the same relative positions shot after shot.

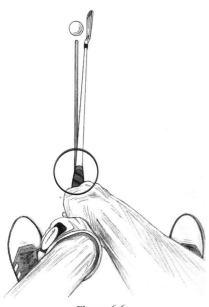

Figure 6.6
**Address for a power club, the ball
about 4 inches inside the left heel.**

We start with a power club—say a 4-iron. Lay a club shaft or dowel on the ground perpendicular to the target line, even with the ball, extending in toward your body. Address the ball, allowing 4 inches between the butt of the club and your body.

Now close your right eye. I want you to address the ball so that the club is flat on its sole, clubface looking at the target, and the shaft positioned so that when you look down out of your left eye, the low end of the grip you are holding "covers" the shaft on the ground, obliterating the lower shaft from sight.

You should address this way with all the power clubs, from the 5-iron through the fairway woods. The driver is a special case, as I will explain.

Figure 6.6 shows what you should see as you look down out of your left eye.

Practice this technique a very great deal, until you can practically set up like this in your sleep—and remember that the more you practice it, the closer you will hit your irons to the hole.

You can practice it at home on the rug, simply placing two shoelaces in the form of a T with the stem of the T pointing at you, a golf ball placed at the intersection of the laces. Practice stepping up with the right foot foremost, squaring the blade, placing the left foot 4 inches left of the shoelace, spreading the right foot, checking the clubface alignment and checking that the grip of the club obliterates the shoelace from sight (with a power club). Check that everything is in place, then step away and start over.

Essentially you are creating a "homing instinct" for an exact address position. And this will do you much more good than hitting buckets of balls at the range.

Once the other variables are taken care of—spine tilt, proper chin position, and so on, you need only follow this procedure, get the shoulders properly aligned (as I will discuss in a moment), and you will have a consistently precise address from shot to shot.

Address with More Lofted Clubs

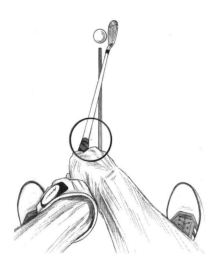

Figure 6.7   Address for a lofted club, the ball about 4 inches inside the left heel.

With the 6-iron through the wedges, the manufacturers construct the club differently, so that when the club is soled properly, the shaft is angled slightly targetward, as seen from the front.

To demonstrate this, take an 8- or 9-iron, set up in the address, look out of your left eye, and put the shaft at such an angle that the low end of the grip you are holding is distinctly on the target side of the shaft you see below it. Figure 6.7 shows how this will look to you.

Practice this also a very great deal, until it is engrained. Students report steady improvement in their games, because the relative positions of ball, clubhead, feet, hands and clubshaft have become stabilized from shot to shot.

Uphill, downhill, and sidehill lies call for adjustments, but these can be made fairly easily once the standard shot off a flat lie has been "molded" in this way for absolute consistency.

Please note that the spine angle never has to change, from the wedge to the driver. The only difference is that with the longer clubs the player stands farther from the ball, as dictated by the lie of the club and the distance from the butt of the club to the player's body.

Driver: A Special Case

I mentioned that the driver was a special case. I recommend that players start out addressing with the driver approximately off the left heel. But because there is a bit more leeway with the driver, I encourage players to "play with it" a bit, addressing the ball a bit forward or backward of that point, to discover what works best for them.

A high percentage of seniors, for instance, are more effective playing the ball slightly more toward the middle of the stance.

I do recommend to all players that they "hover" the driver, that is, don't ground it at address but hold it up opposite the ball, and begin the swing from there. Two of the greatest drivers ever did this—Jack Nicklaus and Greg Norman. It makes for smoother swings, and furthermore it's the rational way to do it. You don't intend to hit the bottom of the tee, so don't address the bottom of the tee.

The Allure of Distance

While we are speaking of driving, there's a lot of talk these days about pros who average over 300 yards off the tee, "launch angles," space-age head and shaft materials, and so on.

Right now this emphasis on distance, distance, distance, is producing a lot of 90-shooters with bad body posture and alignment, who try to push the envelope for distance, and hit the ball into trees, heavy rough, fairway bunkers, and out of bounds.

The pros are getting a lot of distance. But please remember these are very strong young men who already have the body posture and alignment to hit the ball straight, and who are hitting a lot of balls every day, working out in the gym, and are in constant consultation with physical therapists and swing coaches.

For the average player, even in this era of the ball going farther and curving less than it used to, the object should be to get the body angles well-aligned and stable enough, at address and during the swing, so the ball flies down the fairway and gets the hole started successfully.

My players never complain about a lack of distance. They sock the ball quite firmly. But they do it maintaining control of their body angles—that's what gets the ball well out there, and on the fairway.

Shoulder Alignment

We come again to shoulder alignment, which we have been emphasizing from the beginning.

Proper shoulder alignment is sorely needed by the average player, whose shoulder alignment is generally quite *open,* with the right arm riding high at the address, and the right arm very tense. This setup causes a disastrous chain reaction once the swing begins, generally resulting in a slice pattern.

In learning shoulder alignment, it is a great advantage to have already spent a few minutes every day for several weeks performing the spine angle drills that I've described earlier, particularly the "airplane drill" on page 40.

Let's assume that you've spent the requisite time on habituating proper spine angle, both the angle toward the ball and the angle away from the target. The latter tilt sets your shoulders so that the left is distinctly above the level of the right, at address.

The shoulders, as seen from above, should be on the same plane as the target line.

Understand that this alignment is best learned *without hitting balls,* even without holding a club, simply putting your hands in the "prayer" position. Set up, align yourself at a distant target, check for alignment—or have a friend check you—then start over again, without even making a swing.

Work with all the shoulder alignment drills I give you here, find your favorite, and practice it constantly. I tell players, "unless you can align properly, you are *not eligible to hit balls.*"

Here, then, are the drills to work on your shoulder alignment:

The only adjustment I make, according to the player's skill, is that players below about a 5-handicap generally play their best with the shoulders just fractionally open, only about five degrees open. I suggest a trial of this adjustment with my low handicappers, and if they strike the ball better that way, as often happens, I allow them to adopt it. For all others, the shoulders perfectly square is best.

1. Peripheral Vision Drill. Address a ball normally. Keep looking at the ball, don't turn your eyes to the side, but notice, peripherally, whether you can see your right shoulder, then your left shoulder. If your shoulders are properly aligned, you will be able to see both. If your shoulders are too open, you will be able to catch a glimpse of your right shoulder while looking at the ball, but not your left shoulder. That's a dead giveaway that your shoulders are open.

2. Shadow Drill. Get the sun directly in back of you, place a club on the ground pointing to a target off to your left. Take a club and address as if hitting a ball off to that target. Freeze your body position, bring your club up and hold it to your chest. The shadow of the club on your chest should be parallel to the one on the ground, as in Figure 6.8.

3. The Buddy System. This can be done indoors or out, with a club or without. Address a target using a club, or without a club but with the hands in the "prayer" position, palm to palm, fingers pointed at the imaginary ball. Have your friend lay a shaft across your shoulders, and check if they are in plane with the target line.

4. Mirror Drills. Practice addressing an imaginary ball with a mirror to your right,

then with the mirror in front of you, then with the mirror to your left, examining your shoulder position. This can be done indoors without the club as well.

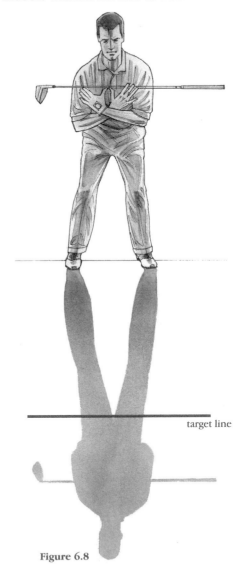

target line

Figure 6.8

I learned a lot about hitting the ball straight from watching the African American cross-handed golfers who came along from the 1930s all the way to the 1950s.

I played in several of the United Golf Association Opens (UGA) in the fifties and sixties as an amateur and saw many of them play. Most were ex-caddies who had picked up the grip in the caddie shed. They were great players. I was impressed with George "Potato Pie" Wallace, and especially with the legendary Howard Wheeler.

Wheeler played most of his golf in stakes games at Cobbs Creek in Philadelphia. He also won a half dozen UGA Opens—at that time the biggest tournament African Americans could play.

Wheeler was the straightest driver I ever saw, straighter than Fred Funk today. And he was long.

Every cross-hander I ever saw in these tournaments was a fine driver—including Charlie Owens, who came along a little later. Getting the ball in play made the game so much easier for them. Because they reached down with the left hand to get it to the lower position, these players tended to address with their shoulders square, rather than open. That's one reason they developed quickly. Most conventional players start out opening their shoulders to get the right hand to its lower place on the shaft—which slows down their development, or stops it altogether.

I believe "left hand low" may be the better way to play the game—but I don't teach it. It's too unconventional for people to accept.

So, even though you play conventionally, learn the lesson that the cross-handers exemplify: when you square your shoulders at address, you make straight hitting much easier.

I told you there would be a great deal to absorb in this chapter, and there is. It must be studied and worked with again and again, until these pre-swing skills are habituated. I admit there is a lot of effort and even tedium involved, but the rewards for your ball striking will be well worth it.

Chapter 7
The Pivot

Once you have perfected your alignment and ball position, you can move on to the second part of preparing to hit full shots, learning the pivot. The pivot is the body motion of the swing, and I teach it independent of the swing itself.

The pivot is one of those areas of golf where what you *think* you're doing may be very different from what you *are* doing. So I emphasize that you use as much objective checking as possible—using a mirror, a practice partner, two chairs, or two clubshafts, as the particular drill shows.

When I first teach the pivot, we learn the motion in a stand-up position, and only after establishing complete freedom of motion do we get into golf posture and "trim" the motion just enough to make it perfect for golf. This is an unusual way of teaching, obviously, but it encourages freedom of motion, and it works. In my lessons, players constantly comment on how well the feelings of the pivot get across to them through this process.

So please stay patient and perform all the drills as you work through this chapter. You'll soon understand what we're trying to do.

There are inherent difficulties in learning a golf pivot. In golf we are swinging at a ball that is beside us and *below the level of our knees.* That's the core of the difficulty.

When we make a level swing, as when we swing at a baseball at chest level, we naturally make a good pivot—we stay well centered and make a good level shoulder turn. But when the object we are striking is below the level of the knees, it's more difficult to turn the shoulders on a level. Some of us have a tendency to tilt the shoulders and begin reverse pivoting, or alternately sway too much and lose our center.

So there are tendencies that you must overcome to get your pivot correct, and we'll discuss them as we go along. The first thing we must check is whether you are susceptible to a reverse pivot.

Start out without a club, with your arms at your sides. Imagine that a very good-looking person is walking behind you to your right, and in a moment will be directly behind you. Turn without lifting your feet off the ground, and look at that person. You will be surprised at the freedom of motion this produces.

More importantly, this initial exercise tells us a great deal about how you will respond to pivoting.

Some People Naturally Reverse Pivot

Photo 7.1
A-pivoter

People turn to look behind them in two distinct ways. We'll call them A and B. In looking behind him to his right, player A moves onto his right leg as he turns (Photo 7.1). *This person will usually get the overall pattern of the pivot quickly,* and it will be a matter of refining his motion and teaching him to make it from a golf posture.

Photo 7.2
B-pivoter

Player B is different. In looking behind him to his right, he keeps his weight on his left side and leans his torso to his left as he looks around him to his right (Photo 7.2). To the observer this may have a "coy" look, but there's nothing affected about it, it's how these people naturally turn, and they are a high percentage of the population, both male and female.

When a player turns this way, I immediately tell him or her, "we have a problem."

I say this because those who turn to look behind them in this fashion are the ones who will have a reverse pivot in their golf swing, and the best way to get them out of that habit in their swings is to change their way of looking behind them, first.

I tell "B-pivoters" that, when they turn to look, I want their weight moving to their right side. Practice with the mirror directly behind you, and turn to look in the mirror as you would turn to look at that attractive person. If you find that you turn in "B" fashion, you must practice turning in the fashion of player A until it feels natural to you, before moving on.

For those who turn like player B, that will take a lot of mirror work. I warned you there might be tendencies that we would have to overcome to get our pivot right. B-pivoters will also be helped by the fact that we teach them to tilt the spine away from the target at address.

My pattern in teaching the pivot is to start with the greatest freedom of motion, and then limit that motion only enough to make it workable in a golf swing. We will start, not in golf posture, but in normal standing posture. Your first drills will be the "Wall" and "Hug Yourself" drills.

Once the player has achieved some proficiency in these drills, I begin to use "hands on" drills, where I physically move parts of the player's body. I suggest you ask a practice partner or spouse to perform my role, which will be clear from the photos.

Imagine that there is a wall in front of you, and place your hands on that wall at about eye level, with the hands about 8 inches apart (Photo 7.3). They should remain 8 inches apart throughout the drill. Don't let your hands get farther apart, or you will be "cheating" and won't benefit from the drill properly.

Now imagine that there is a wall directly behind you. Turn to your right (if you are a right-handed golfer), and put your hands on that imaginary wall, as Photo 7.4 shows. If your left heel tends to come up, let it come up, but don't pick it up deliberately. Next, in one continuous motion, turn to your left and put your hands on the same imaginary wall, but on the other side of you (Photo 7.5).

To do this you swivel the torso and move your weight from your right side to your left, the weight ending on the left leg. You should move freely enough so that at the finish *the only part of the right foot on the ground is the toe.*

Many players are too "tight" at first to pivot freely enough so that the right foot gets on its toe at the finish. I tell them: "release the brake!" They are like a person taking dancing lessons who is too tight to dance properly. If you have difficulty, keep working on *relaxing* until you move right over to the left side and up onto the right toe.

Repeat this exercise in front of a mirror and check the levelness of your shoulder turn.

Photo 7.3

Photo 7.4

Photo 7.5

While standing straight up, hug yourself as in Photo 7.6, each hand on the opposite shoulder. Keeping your head facing forward, turn as you turned when looking behind you to your right (Photo 7.7). You want your weight to move to your right side, and end with your chest facing an imaginary wall to your right. You should feel also that your chest is *over your right leg,* and your left shoulder is almost over your right knee. Then rotate your body to your left until you arrive on the flat of your left foot and on the toe of your right foot (Photo 7.8).

Photo 7.6   Photo 7.7   Photo 7.8

Hug yourself at address, then have your partner hold one of your shoulders in each hand, as in Photo 7.9, and physically turn you to the right, making your shoulders turn level (Photo 7.10). Then have your partner "turn you to the target" as I am doing in Photo 7.11, by rotating your shoulders.

Another version of this exercise, not photographed here, is to have the partner wind you up as in Photo 7.10, then, keeping his left hand on your right shoulder, reach down with his right hand, placing it on the inside of your left knee, then send the left knee to the target at the same time that he rotates your right shoulder toward the target with his left hand.

Photo 7.9

Photo 7.10

Photo 7.11

A third version, shown in Photos 7.12 to 7.14, is to have the partner stand behind you with a hand on each of your hips, then rotate you to a top-of-swing position, then rotate you to a finish, making sure that your hips turn level. In each case you should arrive at a finishing position on the flat of your left foot and the toe of your right foot.

Photo 7.12   Photo 7.13   Photo 7.14

Spread your arms out in the form of a letter T (Photo 7.15), rotate to your right (Photo 7.16), and then to your left (Photo 7.17).

Photo 7.15   Photo 7.16   Photo 7.17

Learning the Overall Movement of the Pivot

I use several variations of these drills, moving different parts of the body until the pivot feels like *one unified motion,* even though in reality a number of body parts are moving.

I generally find that, when I first give these drills to a player, his or her weight tends to move too much to the outside of the right foot going back. That's acceptable at an early stage, because we want to start with maximum freedom of motion.

Trimming the Pivot

Once you've done enough work to get the feeling of the pivot, our next step is to refine the foot and leg action. Hug yourself, and as you turn your shoulders back, keep your weight on the inside of your right heel. Then, as you turn forward with your shoulders, feel the weight go to the outside of the left heel as you come up on your right toe. Work on this with a mirror.

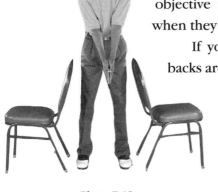

You must also self-check to make sure you're not swaying. This is one of those details where you must get objective feedback, because swayers generally can't tell when they are swaying.

If you are indoors, set up two chairs so that their backs are right next to your hips, with only an inch or two of clearance.

Place your hands in "prayer" position (Photo 7.18), and swing back (Photo 7.19) and through as if you had a golf club. You should be able to do so without hitting either chair with your legs and hips—although at the finish (Photo 7.20), you

Photo 7.18

Photo 7.19

Photo 7.20

should be on a vertical left leg, and very close to the chair on your left, even nudging it.

If you slide into the right chair going back, or slide into the left one going through enough to move it, work with the chairs until you don't disturb them. If you are outdoors, you can stick dowels or broken golf shafts in the ground so that the upper parts of the shafts abut your hips.

With some players this can take some work. If you have trouble, it helps to imagine a rod passing straight down through your head and the middle of your body, and try to revolve around that rod.

Check in the mirror, also, to make sure your shoulders don't dip as you pivot.

It helps a great deal to have already habituated the "chin up" position, and the tilt of the spine away from the target at address. If you are having trouble with swaying, make sure these two angles are well ingrained.

A technique I've used very successfully is to switch roles—I have the player work my shoulder and knee to make me pivot. Players report that this helps them tremendously, I think because they get more of a visual idea of how the pivot works.

It is also very important to check on the stability of your body angles during your pivoting practice. That is, when you draw back the triangle of arms and shoulders, the angle of the right knee should stay the same, and the spine angle should stay the same.

Work on this a good deal with no club, hands in the prayer position, and a mirror on your right. It also helps to get a sturdy table behind you, and to adopt an address position where your rear is backed up against it. With the hands in prayer position make a backswing, and you will be able to feel clearly whether you stay "centered."

That is, your rump will either slide to the right along the table (incorrect) or your hips will rotate and your right buttock will roll along the table. You will also see clearly the importance of the right knee angle staying stable.

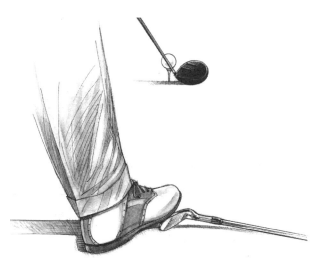

Figure 7.1 **Right foot with club wedged beneath. Practice swinging without a club, then eventually with a club and hitting balls.**

If you have trouble with the angle of the right knee changing, it's helpful to wedge the head of an iron club underneath the right foot, as shown in Figure 7.1, and make swings with the hands in prayer position, or with a club. This forces you to stay on the inside of the right foot and maintain the knee angle.

Obviously this chapter gives you a great deal to work on. Please don't think you'll read it and acquire good pivoting habits in a day or two. It takes time—especially if you are a B-pivoter. It would be a good idea to assign yourself 10 minutes of drilling a day until you start to get a really good pivot. If you get on the golf course and have to remind yourself to pivot, or think consciously about any details of your pivot, *you haven't prepared enough.* Do more work without a club, and you'll perform much better with a club.

I'm sure you are asking, as perhaps you have all along, "when do I get to hit balls?" The answer is, not quite yet.

Once we have prepared our ball position, alignment, and pivot, we do not move on to full shots yet, but instead "round out" the elements of the swing by uniting the arm and body motion, and getting the overall movement of our components in sync.

We are helped by the fact that we have been working on our angles all along.

- Because we have worked on keeping our chin well up and pointed to the right of the ball, we can make a full shoulder turn with comparative ease.

- Because we employ a proper spine tilt toward the ball and to our right, we can coil fully in the backswing without fear of reverse pivoting.

- Because we've learned to align with our shoulders square at address, we tend to swing on the proper path, rather than the slicer's or hooker's path.

- Because we keep the right knee angle stable, we tend to keep our spine angle consistent, so we hit the ball much more squarely instead of fat or thin.

We will continue to work on these angles during the final part of the book, where our overall purpose is to blend the body motion we have learned with our arm, wrist and hand motion into coordinated movement.

The drills and explanations in the following pages will help you achieve these objectives. You can work on most of these drills alone. However when we are coordinating the parts of your body in the swing, it is extremely helpful, even necessary, to work with a spouse or friend who mimics what I do in the photos. The person performing this function doesn't need to be "golf savvy," he or she simply needs to reproduce what I'm doing.

Incidentally, these coordination drills are often the most fun for players, because they produce the Eureka! feeling of "now I know what a unified swing feels like."

First we must establish the connection between arm swing and the movement of the torso.

Chapter 8
Connection: The Blend of Arm and Body Movement

To blend arm and body movement, we establish the habits of (1) letting the right elbow hinge easily in the backswing, and (2) maintaining an adherence of the upper left arm to the torso until the ball is struck. These are our keys to "connection."

The Easily Hinging Right Elbow

Most golfers have no idea of the importance of getting the right elbow to fold easily in the backswing. This allows the player to retain center while the body coils.

When the right elbow resists bending, the player begins swaying during the backswing, losing "center," and the swing can never recover its plane.

Take the time to demonstrate to yourself this all-important difference. You won't need a club, only a sturdy table at about the level of your rear end. Address an imaginary ball with an imaginary club, with your buttocks backed up against the edge of the table, as you did a few pages ago, when practicing pivoting. Your hands are in the prayer position.

Start to make a backswing motion, and as you do so be sure that your right elbow folds easily. Also, as you make this backswing, monitor

117

your right knee and make sure it retains the same degree of flex, and also feel your right buttock rolling on the table edge as your hips turn— note that your rump does not slide to the right along the table edge.

That's the way it should take place in the swing.

Now let's experience the wrong chain reaction. Get in the same address position, and as you make a backswing, deliberately tense up your right arm and shoulder, so the right elbow will resist folding. At the same time, deliberately slide to your right along the table edge. This is the reaction that takes place when there is too much tension in the right side at address.

When the right elbow resists folding, the entire body sways to the right, and the player cannot swing the club on plane.

In making sure that your right elbow bends easily, the best place to start is with square shouldered alignment and relaxation of your right arm at address.

Practice the correct way repeatedly, until maintaining center, allowing your right elbow to bend easily, and maintaining stability with the right knee, all feel like one move, even though several parts are moving.

Adhesion of Upper Left Arm to the Torso

Now for the second part of combining the arms with the torso— establishing the adhesion between the upper left arm and the ribcage.

I remember one of the first players I taught to get "connected" in this way. My student, Jack, was an insurance man just getting into golf. He obviously wasn't getting the most out of his athletic ability. He had lettered in several sports in college, but had only played golf for four years, and was a 12-handicap.

I explained to Jack that if he could establish more connection between his arms and his body, he would graduate to a different class as a player. To illustrate my point I actually tied his upper arms to his sides with rope, and had him hit a batch of balls. He quickly began hitting the ball better, and went to work on his connection. At the end of 12 months he was hovering around a 3-handicap, and stayed there for the next 25 years.

Countless times with my students, making the connection between arms and body has paved the way to much lower scores. The key to gaining this connection is the adhesion of the upper left arm, in particular.

Let's establish again a clear sense of contrast between the right way and the wrong way, and give you a drill for connection. Stand in your normal golf address, with an imaginary ball and club, but holding the imaginary club in your left hand only. Keep your right hand at your side or behind your back. Keeping your chest facing forward, not rotating it to the right or left at all, make a backswing and forward swing with your left arm alone.

Notice how awkward it feels. You feel that your arm is unsupported, it's flipping and flopping around. This is disconnection, and most golfers play with some degree of disconnection between arm movement and body movement.

Now let's show the correct way, and this is a drill you can use again and again. Adopt the same address position, and make your upper left arm adhere to your ribcage, as if you were holding something there—such as a handkerchief. Make a nice easy swing of the left arm, back and through (Photos 8.1, 8.2, and 8.3 on the next page). Notice that in the follow through the handkerchief would drop to the ground. That is, you don't maintain the adherence after the imaginary ball is struck.

Use this drill a great deal, and you will get the close integration of arm motion and body motion that the good player has. The sensation is that the arms are riding the body turn. There's a feeling of "everything moving at once," and we're going to enhance that feeling even more in the ensuing chapter.

Photo 8.1   Photo 8.2   Photo 8.3

The "Feel" of the Overall Swing

We're now ready to further our "connectedness" by using drills to teach unity of motion—drills where we feel the full swing—and for my pupils I want this to be a *non-verbal* experience. That is, I teach players through drills, not through explanation. In fact I think there are too many words and explanations already!

Golfers continually ask questions such as:

"What begins the backswing?"

"What begins the downswing?"

"Do the arms control the body, or does the body control the arms?"

"When do I break my wrists in my takeaway?" and so on.

The way I teach, we don't need such discussions. Instead, we put the player in position to feel one component, then two components, then several components of a good swing simultaneously. How the player interprets this feel with the conscious mind is his or her own business, but I want to make sure the subconscious absorbs the *whole* integrated motion.

Remember, golfers feel the swing differently—and they "key" on different things. For that matter, if you asked three baseball pitchers what they "keyed on" during the delivery motion, you would probably get three different answers.

Many of the longest-running arguments in golf are futile, because in reality they are disputes about how different people feel the same thing.

For example: "What begins the downswing?" Sam Snead felt it as the left hand and arm pulling the butt of the club down like a bell pull. Byron Nelson felt it as the left knee moving toward the target. Bobby Jones and Ben Hogan felt it as the hips turning. Tommy Armour felt it as the right knee moving toward the ball.

The truth is that, in a good downswing, all those things occur. But these great players had different brains, different physiologies, and they felt things differently.

If you are an instructor, you are mistaken if you try to make the player feel things *your* way.

My students ask questions, but I don't even get drawn into a discussion of this kind. Instead I help the pupil build up the feel of a good swing through as many components as I can. This is done without holding a club or striking a ball. The student works only with the triangle and body movement.

Finally, after a lot of this work, I allow the student to take hold of a club and strike a shot. And we find that the components we have worked on "engage" as soon as he draws the club back. And the player strikes the ball very well.

I realize some readers will say, "this Richardson fellow spends pages and pages telling me how to train myself to chip and putt, how to align, how to get good posture, how to pivot, and then spends only a few pages discussing the motion of the swing! What is wrong with him? This is a golf book. Shouldn't we have an extended discussion of the swing?"

The answer is no. The way I teach, *preparation controls motion*.

You train yourself, and train yourself, and train yourself, without hitting balls, and when you get the club in your hands, you let your training take over.

There should be no voice in your mind saying, "what do I do first, what do I do second?" You get up to strike the ball, and your subconscious takes over, because it's been trained.

So when a player asks me questions like "What begins the downswing?" I say, "By the time we get to that, you will find that it has already been taken care of." And that's exactly how it turns out.

Remember, a good golfer is a good golfer partly because he knows *what not to think about.* And a good golf teacher is a good golf teacher partly because he knows *what not to talk about.*

Bench Drills

Our next step is to begin drills for connected motion in the swing, where all the essential parts of the body move simultaneously. I refer to them as "bench drills," because for some of them I sit in front of the player on a bench. Some of them are similar to the drills for the pivot, but with the arms involved. I'm assuming that you have already had practice swinging with the left arm alone, with no club, and with the upper left arm adhering to the torso.

Also, please realize that you can't learn this lesson alone. You must actually have someone do what I am doing in the photos.

Perhaps the best way to explain bench drills is to show exactly what I do with pupils, and your partner can help you in a similar fashion. First, I tell the student to address an imaginary ball with an imaginary club, with hands and arms in the prayer position. I remind the student to be sure that the upper left arm adheres to the rib cage.

I tell the player to incline the body weight slightly toward the insteps. In my lesson I then gently nudge the knees toward each other, which helps make leg and foot work more compact.

I tell the player to move as if to shake hands left-handed with an imaginary person to his right. Then I ask, "Did you notice how your left knee moved, when you did that?"

I want the player to comment on this. The left knee should move toward a point slightly to the right of the imaginary ball being struck, as the player sees it, and the torso should rotate to the right. In photo 8.4, you see me gently pushing the left knee into its proper position.

Once the student is in this "shaking hands" position, with the left arm approximately horizonal, I simultaneously move the player's left knee toward the imaginary target and move the right knee toward the imaginary ball. This sends the player right through to a finish, as pictured (Photos 8.5, 8.6, 8.7).

Students always seem to enjoy this exercise, because it gives them a sense of unity of motion in the swing. We then go back to the address. Students make the "shaking hands" backswing, then I move just the left knee toward the target, and everything else goes along to the finish. We perform these drills enough so players get used to the sequence of motion—the weight moves toward the target, a little gap opens up between the knees, then the right knee catches up, as the body rotates toward the target. They don't force any of these things, or even consciously analyze them, they just feel them.

Photo 8.4

Photo 8.5

Photo 8.6   Photo 8.7

Next, the player makes the same backswing, and I place my left hand on his right shoulder, my right hand on the inside of his right knee, and "unwind" the shoulder at the same time that I send the left knee at the target—again the player moves right through to the finish.

Then I get behind the player, have him make the same backswing, then I put one hand on each hip, and turn the player manually. Again the player pivots right through to the finish.

With enough of these drills, the player begins to feel that, as soon as one part of the body gets in motion in the swing, all parts of the body relevant to the swing will get in motion, and they will be coordinated with each other.

This is what the great swingers feel when swinging—Gene Littler, Tommy Bolt, Mickey Wright, Sam Snead, Ernie Els. The handicap player can start to get some of these feelings with a little manual assistance, and he or she can carry on from there.

I also recommend that you close your eyes for some of these swings. This makes the feelings more vivid, and easier to learn.

The Striking Motion

In my experience, the more work my students do on blending the arm motion and body motion, the better they strike the ball and the better they score.

My favorite drill to achieve this is what I call the chop drill, combined with the hug yourself pivot drill you have already learned. The chop is a variation of an old Scottish drill that's been used for a hundred years or more. It was promoted by professionals Peter Croker and Jeff Johnson.

I teach the chop at first without the club, only adding the club at a later stage.

SKILL BUILDER *Chop Drill*

Put your right hand in the "tray" position near your right ear, the palm about 45° from vertical (Photo 8.8). Position the left hand as shown in Photo 8.9, the back of the left hand in line with the left forearm. From there make a motion with your arms downward and to the left, as if delivering a two-handed karate chop to an object just to the left of your left hip (Photos 8.10 and 8.11).

Photo 8.8

Photo 8.9

Photo 8.10

Photo 8.11

Hug yourself as in the pivot drills (Photo 8.12), and coil to the right into a "top of backswing" position (Photo 8.13). Keeping your torso in that position, put your right hand in the "tray" position, place the left hand on (Photo 8.14)—then make the chopping drill down and to your left, and simply let the body go along (Photo 8.15). Stay loose, don't tense up, and your body should keep turning as your weight moves onto your left leg. You should arrive at a finishing position with your body facing the imaginary target, your weight on the flat of your left foot and on the toe of your right foot (Photo 8.16).

Photo 8.12   Photo 8.13   Photo 8.14   Photo 8.15   Photo 8.16

Don't make the chop motion longer or more complicated than you see in the pictures. Remember, the point of the drill isn't how *much* hand and wrist motion you need, but how *little* you need, once it is combined with the pivot.

Perform the chop drill at least fifty or sixty times before combining it with the "hug and pivot, then chop drill" on the facing page.

In reality the golf swing is just the chop drill combined with the pivot, and that's the combination we are learning.

Repeated use of these drills will help you make a simpler and more repetitive swing motion, with a "live" pivot and with no extra movement with the forearms and hands.

Transition to Hitting Full Shots

At this point, you are free to begin hitting full shots. As my players are doing so, I look them over and work out any kinks in their games. Perhaps they're standing too far from the ball, or their shoulder alignment is a bit off, etc. We correct those problems, if any, but these are merely adjustments.

However, there are two drills that are especially helpful as they make the transition to striking balls. These are (1) using the left hand alone to hit tees with the butt of the club, and (2) going from a horizontal "baseball style" swing to a golf swing.

Take a middle iron, and address an imaginary ball hanging in the air beside you at about shoulder level. Make a level swing at that ball like a baseball swing. You can feel how easy it is to maintain center, and make a good level shoulder turn. Swing that way for 10 or 20 very easy swings.

You should notice that, in addition to your good "centeredness" and pivot, as your club passes through the impact area you are rotating the toe of the club easily over its heel. You sense the flow of the club head as it swings. You should also notice that, as you swing back, your right elbow folds easily, and as you swing through, your left elbow folds easily. All these factors are very important in the golf swing.

As you repeat these swings, incline your swing more and more as if you are swinging at a ball that is getting lower and lower, and eventually is on the ground. Make sure that your swing retains the characteristics I've spoken of above—you keep your center, make a level shoulder turn, make sure the toe of the club is rotating properly past the heel swinging through, and allow the left elbow to bend in the follow through just as the right elbow bent going back. Feel the flowing motion of the club head as it swings.

The drill is very simple. Take a club in the left hand alone, holding it by the shaft near the head end instead of the grip end (Photo 8.17). Place tees in the ground in a line perpendicular to the target line, and simply address and strike them with a left-armed swing (Photos 8.18, 8.19. This gets you in the habit of addressing and swinging to actually strike an object, but it doesn't put the pressure on you that hitting golf balls does.

Photo 8.17   Photo 8.18   Photo 8.19

Chapter 9
The Full Swing

At this point you are ready to hit full shots, practice at the range, and play rounds of golf.

As I warn my students who are starting to hit balls, you can't expect perfect performance, especially if you have been changing long-standing habits. You must learn to ignore individual miscues—don't take them to heart—the main thing is that your game as a whole is moving forward.

I also give my students individual checkpoints in the swing, so they can make sure they are on the right track. You can work with these too.

"Eight O'Clock" Checkpoint

The first point I call the 8 o'clock position (from the player's point of view it is the 2 o'clock position) at the mid-point of the takeaway.

Assume your normal stance for a middle iron shot, and place an extra club on the ground so that its shaft passes from the inside of your left heel to the toe of your right foot, then extends outward and to your right, toward 2 o'clock as you see it.

Using a middle iron, make a normal address and swing back to the point where the shaft of the club you are swinging is directly

Photo 9.1 Eight o'clock

over the shaft you have placed on the ground—and stop there (see photo 9.1). Note that the shafts are not parallel—one of them merely "covers" the other, as seen by you, the player. Check that (1) your clubhead is still low to the ground and hasn't been picked up, (2) your left shoulder has begun to turn, (3) your right knee is stable.

"Nine O'Clock" Checkpoint

The second checkpoint—what I call the 9 o'clock position—is well into the takeaway. It is the first time in the swing that the shaft of the club passes through a horizontal position. Take your stance for a middle iron shot, then place an extra club on the ground to your right, parallel to the target line, the butt of the club about two inches from the outside of your right foot, opposite the ball of the foot.

Make your takeaway, and stop when the clubshaft is over the club on the ground, as you see it (Photo 9.2).

Check to make sure the butt of the club you are swinging is directly above the butt of the club on the ground. If the butt of the club you are swinging is much closer to your body, you are failing to get proper extension. If the butt of the club you are swinging is much farther out, you are forc-

position of club on ground

Photo 9.2 Nine o'clock

Better Golf: A Skill Building Approach

ing the club outward, and losing "connection." Modify your action accordingly.

Also check to make sure that at this point in the swing your thumbs are on their way to pointing up, which means you are swinging the club back in the proper plane.

Check also that the left shoulder is continuing its turn, and the right arm is folding easily at the elbow.

Top of the Swing Checkpoint

It's also helpful to check the top-of-swing position with a mirror to your right. Make a backswing (Photo 9.3), stop at the most advanced point of your swing. It doesn't need to be "parallel"—that will depend on your flexibility. Check to make sure that (1) your weight has moved to the inside of your right foot, (2) your right knee angle has remained stable, (3) your spine angle has been maintained.

Also, the clubshaft should pass either directly over your right shoulder or over the higher part of your right bicep.

Check also the position of your hands and wrists. The back of the left hand should be in line with the left forearm, and the wrists should be under the shaft.

Those checkpoints are extremely helpful. I also like to give my students drills they can use to reinforce the rhythm and movement of the overall swing, as described on the following pages.

Photo 9.3 Top of the swing. Depending on flexibility, that may be three-quarters length, as shown, or all the way to parallel (dotted line). Stay "connected," and don't force the length of the backswing.

Stand upright with your feet shoulder width apart, arms out in the form of a T (Photo 9.4). Your movement in this drill will be one continuous, rhythmic motion.

Rotate your shoulders to the right until they have turned about 90 degrees (Photo

9.5). As your shoulders are still finishing their turn, put your hands in the chopping position above your right shoulder (Photo 9.6), then make the chopping motion downward and to your left (Photo 9.7), allowing the body to "go along." You should continue to rotate to your left and move your weight to your left side, until you finish in a position on the flat of your left foot and the toe of your right foot (Photo 9.8).

In this drill the plane of your arm swing going back is level, the plane of your arm swing coming forward is about 45 degrees down from level—but don't let this concern you, just make a rhythmic, continuous motion. My students report extremely good results from this drill.

Photo 9.4

Photo 9.5   Photo 9.6   Photo 9.7   Photo 9.8

To help streamline and simplify hand and wrist motion in the downswing, it is also helpful to practice the "butt of the club at the target line" drill.

Perform this drill with easy swings only, using a middle iron, and hitting shots no more than 100 yards.

Address the ball normally, make a ⅔ backswing, then start the downswing by getting the butt of the club pointed at the target line (see photos 9.9 and 9.10), then swinging through from there. The part of the swing going from the photo on the left to the photo on the right should feel almost like the release of a slingshot, with no extra "steering" or manipulation of the hands. The sensation I want students to get is, "I got the butt of the club on the target line, and the next thing I knew the ball was gone."

It's true that some pros object to this drill, so I should explain my position on it.

Dissenting pros feel that, since most golfers slice by leaving the clubface open at contact, the student trying to "lead with the butt of the club" will only leave the clubface more open, and slice worse.

That doesn't happen with my pupils, because I've prepared them beforehand—they've learned the proper position of the chin and head, they've learned to rotate the club, they've learned to address with the shoulders square. So when they get the butt of the club pointing at the target line, they don't leave the clubface open or "block it out," they release the club properly, and the ball flies off toward the target—not to the right.

Photo 9.9   Photo 9.10

Keeping the Swing Going
(Even with the Ball There)

One warning I give my students who have been preparing their games and are now striking shots is not to allow the ball to make them tense. I want them to keep up the same level of relaxation they had when the ball wasn't there. I realize this is easier said than done.

I like to tell players, "release your brakes!"

Try to remember that the ball has no resistance. It's an ounce and a half of rubber. If you weigh as much as the average golfer, you are 1500 times the weight of the golf ball. It will offer no more resistance than a piece of tissue paper. Ask yourself, what would happen if you swung through a square of tissue paper, instead of a golf ball? Your arms would relax. Your body would relax. Let them relax.

Final Review of the Six Angles

Our last step in discussing the full swing is to review the six angles with which we began, and see how those angles will control even the powerful motion of the drive.

As I said early in this book, our purpose was to develop a "delivery motion," almost like the motion of a bowler, with consistent pace and control of body angles. With some of my students this motion is so powerful that it results in 290-yard drives. With less powerful students, it may result in 160-yard drives. But the point is that the motion in both cases is controlled, and results in a high percentage of fairways hit.

Let's review how the six angles will give you this control.

Angles number 1, number 2 and number 3 are the spine angle toward the ball, the spine angle to your right, and the alignment of the shoulders in plane with the target line. I lump these three together because they work in conjunction to effectively position the torso in the anatomically proper position for swinging a club.

Angle number 1   Angle number 2   Angle number 3

Over 90% of golfers limit their development through incorrect position of the torso at address—the most common mistakes being open shoulders, stooped-over posture and a lean of the torso toward the target. If the torso is in the wrong position, the arms cannot swing the club on the proper plane, because the joints from which the arms are swinging are mispositioned.

When the torso is properly aligned, and the grip is good, and the arms are relaxed, you can swing the arms and club freely back and forth, and the clubhead will tend to true up at contact.

That doesn't mean that you will hit every ball perfectly. Far from it. Golf is a difficult game, and you are a human being, subject to error.

But if you believe in what you are doing, you will accept the individual miscues, and trust that, as you work on your game, the proportion of good shots will keep getting better—as it will.

The number 4 angle is the stable angle of the right knee in the backswing, which allows you to keep the spine and torso in the proper plane as you swing.

A special word about this angle, because many of my students must make a point of working at it. Right knee angle, like spine

Angle number 4

angle, is a particularly difficult "self check." What you feel you're doing is not necessarily what you're doing. Place a mirror to your right, make practice backswings (with or without a club), look in the mirror and check this angle.

On this subject, a student recently came to me saying he had watched films of Sam Snead, and Snead's right knee did straighten slightly during the backswing. To me this is allowable—a slight straightening where the knee remains well flexed. But once that right knee straightens to the point where the spine begins to react and straighten, all stability in the spine angle is lost. And this problem is extremely common among handicap players.

Many powerful players subconsciously sense that they can turn more when they straighten up out of the spine angle. While they might succeed in turning more, they lose spine angle stability, and the ball flies all over the place. Once I get them to stabilize the right knee and spine angles, they may feel more restricted for a time,

Angle number 5

but they soon learn to coil powerfully in the new position. The results are far greater consistency in ball striking, and lower scores.

The number 5 angle is the angle of the head and chin at address and during the backswing, with the chin well up and pointed to the right of the ball. This angle is important primarily because it makes the proper spine angle so much easier to set up and maintain. Once the chin drops, everything goes wrong. The shoulders are prevented from turning, and they begin to tilt. The result? Lack of coil, reverse pivoting, and weak slices.

Some players complain to me, "I'm right eye dominant," or "I'm not comfortable turning my head," etc. If you are in this category, let me guarantee you that you can

138

become more comfortable than you think. It's also helpful to demonstrate to yourself the benefits—then you'll have more patience with the change.

To do this you need only a pillow and a wall, not even a club. Adopt a normal address position with your hands in prayer position, with the wall close in front of you. Place the pillow between your head and the wall so that, when you stand at address, the very top of your head is pinning the pillow against the wall. This sets up a very "head down" address position, your chin tight to your chest.

Make a backswing motion, and you will immediately sense how your body locks up, and can't coil properly.

Now, adopt the same address, but "pin" the pillow with the part of your head right at your hairline, and on the left side of your forehead. Your chin is now well up, and pointing to the right of the imaginary ball. There is a good distance between your chin and your chest.

Make a backswing. Your freedom of motion, and the ease with which you coil, are evident. That freedom means more power, as well as a better spine angle. It is worth an initial period of discomfort to get used to a "chin well up and to the right" address position.

Angle number 6 is the easily-increasing angle of the right elbow, which allows the swing to come to the inside during the backswing, and allows you to maintain "center."

When the above six angles are all working in the swing at the same time, they control the "flow" of the swing and its direction of movement—straight away from the ball, then moving easily to the inside and up over the right shoulder, then flowing into and through the ball from the inside. So the swing really does become an effective "delivery motion" that gets the ball in the fairway time after time.

And when your game goes wrong, as it occasionally will, don't hit ball after ball trying to "hit your way back

Angle number 6

into form." Instead, go back to your address position. Go back to your mirror. Check your ball position and alignment. Review these six angles—you should find yourself coming around.

This concludes our work on the swing. I will spend the final chapters of the book discussing three subjects: (1) how this learning method helps you to overcome some of the long-standing problems in golf, (2) how to maintain your game now that you are playing on a better level, and (3) how to keep your attitude positive once you get on the golf course.

Chapter 10
Why My Students Don't Slice Anymore

If you work diligently with this book, you start to realize how using these drills to change your habits can solve some of the most common problems in golf.

Overcoming Three Problems

I'll talk about just three of these common problems—slicing, wild hitting, and inept short game shots.

Slicing

If you have any background in golf, you realize this is the number one problem for the majority of players. All golfers seem to begin their careers as slicers and then modify their technique to hit the ball straight—some successfully, others less so.

As established in this book, most of the problems that produce slicing begin *before the club is swung.* The most common address problem that causes the slice is the open shoulders-tense right shoulder-tense right arm-high right arm problem.

To make this issue clear, let's exaggerate some of the slicer's traits to the point of caricature. We exaggerate, but many of you

Photo 10.1   Photo 10.2

slicers will find that the resulting caricature reminds you of your physical feelings at address. Then we'll show the correct way.

From the overhead shot in Photo 10.1, you can see the classic alignment of the slicer, with the shoulders wide open. But in the second photo, we've also added the tension that gets into the right shoulder, resulting in a position that looks like the player is trying to touch his right shoulder to his ear (Photo 10.2). This is the slicer's address turned into a caricature: If you happen to be a slicer, stand up to an imaginary ball and deliberately adopt this address, canting the shoulders wide open, raising the right shoulder, and tensing up the right arm for good measure. These positions may seem like mere exaggerations of your normal address traits, and because they are exaggerated, you can feel clearly what your problem is.

You can also feel how difficult it is to make a proper backswing, straight back from the ball and then to the inside. There is such a mountain of tension in that right shoulder and arm that the swing can't come inside going back. The only thing possible is to come "over the top" and slice the ball.

Now let's see the changes that the slicer must make, and which will result from using the drills in this book.

Better Golf: A Skill Building Approach

Photo 10.3

Photo 10.4

First, we change the angle of the shoulders from the incorrect open alignment (Photo 10.3) to the proper alignment in plane with the target line (Photo 10.4). I have placed a board under the arms to make clear the plane of the shoulders and the arms.

Second, let's relax and lower that right shoulder. Just imagine that I'm placing a hand on your shoulder and saying "relax that shoulder, relax, relax, relax . . ." and slowly your shoulder is going down and down and getting more relaxed. And I also want your right arm "soft," not tense, and I want that right elbow ready to fold very easily when the club is drawn back.

Now the swing has someplace to go. It can go straight back and then to the inside—nothing is blocking it. So we can coil powerfully and swing at the ball from the inside, instead of coming over the top.

If you are a customary slicer, imitate this caricature, and then imitate the correction. You'll find out a lot about why you are slicing in the first place, and what to do about it. But to make the correction permanent, you must work with the drills in this book, persistently and over time.

Wild Hitting

Another common problem that we see every day on the course is the wild or uncontrolled hitter who hits the ball all over the place. The cliche about this player is that he or she "air mails the ball but doesn't know the zip code."

There seems to be an acceptance of the idea that people who are wild will just continue to be wild—that it's something in their nature, or their genes or something. I don't buy that. I have worked with many wild hitting golfers and taught them to hit the ball straight.

Let's say I have a wild hitting male golfer who hits it 270 yards or 280 yards, but all over the place. We start to work on his posture and alignment angles. At first it may seem restrictive for him to stay within those angles at the address, and keep the right knee flexed during the backswing, not rise up as he turns, keep his chin well up and pointed right and get his shoulder alignment correct—these things may feel slightly restrictive, though in reality they are freeing him to make a better swing.

But because he's self-conscious (which slows down movement) he only hits the ball, let's say, 240 for a while, while we're working. But! The ball is heading straight down the fairway all the time, because those body angles are being controlled. The big slice, the big pull, the big hook, the big push—those are gone.

And as he gets used to operating within the proper body angles and alignments, and as his muscles relax more and more, without his trying to make the club move faster, it moves faster. The 240 becomes 250, which becomes 255, which becomes 260. He may or may not eventually hit the ball as far as with his original motion. But whether he does or not, he's delighted, because he's controlling the ball so much better, not only off the tee, but with the fairway clubs. His shot dispersion is narrowing, and that always makes the game so much easier.

It is a myth that the wild hitter must always be wild. In truth he is a wild hitter because body angles are changing inappropriately, or getting out of control, or have been set wrongly at the address to begin with. When the body angles are brought into discipline, the change for the better in directional control can be amazing.

Bad Short Game Shots

The third common problem is wasteful short game sequences. For example, the player steps up to a simple 30-foot chip and knocks the ball 10 feet past, or 10 feet short of the hole. With practice of the ladder drill, this kind of wasteful, "touch of an elephant" shot becomes more and more rare.

Another common example of "short game waste" is the so-called tricky shot, for instance the short shot over a bunker to the flag. Inept players flip at the shot with their hands, trying to lift the ball over the bunker, resulting in either fat or bladed shots—which hurts their scores and their self-confidence (Photo 10.5).

On the other hand, if you have worked with the drills in this book, you have several factors working in your favor when you prepare to strike this shot.

First, the "flipping" has been trained out of your stroke. You stroke with the triangle, which makes things a lot easier on your nerves. Also, because you've practiced extensively with the second ball 12 inches behind the ball that you strike, you're more confident your clubhead will come in at the correct angle to get a crisp strike (Photo 10.6).

From ladder drill practice, you sense that this particular shot should be struck with the strength of about a 50-foot putt. With all these factors working in your favor, the fear of the bunker is gone—it might as well not be there.

Photo 10.5   The untrained player flips the clubhead forward with his hands.

Photo 10.6   The finish of a good chipping stroke, resulting from drills in this book. The clubhead has passed the hands only after the ball has been struck. The right knee has moved with the stroke, easing the body action.

Your attention is solely on how the ball will react once it lands on the green, because you're confident you can land it there. Now it's a question of touch—like a lag putt.

Can you see how far you have advanced? You're thinking about getting the ball close to the hole. The untrained, "handsy" player is worrying about getting the ball over the bunker. You are thinking and performing more like a touring pro, rather than a middle- or upper-handicap golfer. And over time, your results will reflect it.

So you see that some of the most common problems of golf—slicing, wild hitting, wasting shots in the short game—start to disappear as you train yourself in cumulative skills.

Again, this is not a quick process. It takes time and persistence to learn these skills. There are likely to be bad habits that you must overcome, which takes extra work. But at the end of it all is a far more efficient way of getting a ball around a golf course, with the minimum of "bad holes" and the maximum of enjoyment. Your time commitment is eminently worth it.

Chapter 11
Maintaining Your Game

Players who have worked through my standard half dozen lessons find that their games have reached a better level. But they need to know how to "maintain." Here's what to work on to keep your game "going," or even improving.

- Work on your weaknesses. Most golfers practice their strengths, because they flatter them and make them look good to those practicing around them. But is that the object of practice? You should be shoring up your weaknesses.

  Tom Kite is a great example of a player who worked on his weaknesses, and kept getting better and better. Ben Hogan was once asked why he rarely seemed to practice pitching wedge shots. Hogan replied that the pitching wedge had always been the easiest club in the bag for him—and he preferred to practice the shots that he found tougher.

- Practice away from the golf course, and even during your daily life. This is important, because so many golfers feel that they "don't have the time" to devote to improvement. But in reality they do.

  Let's say, for instance, you commute 30 minutes to work.

While driving or riding you can hold golf tees between your thumbs and forefingers. Or think about the feeling of the banking airplane drill, or the feeling of your shoulders being aligned squarely.

My students report great success with this technique. They find that "thinking about how the drill feels" does almost as much good as performing the drill itself.

- When drilling at home or in the office, close your eyes for part of your drill time. It has been long established by the best teaching pros that students learn better when they do this—it makes them feel more vividly.

- Practice drills on posture continuously. Particularly important are the drills on spine angle—inclination forward (the one-legged drill), and away from the target (the banking airplane drill).

- Practice standing on one leg for a minute or more each day—balance needs to be tuned (Photo 11.1).

- Work on the hold of the club and rotation, especially if you are a mid- to upper-handicapper or tend to slice the ball. Practice finger curls, practice holding golf tees or blades of grass between thumbs and forefingers, practice the windshield wiper drill.

- Practice swinging the driver and 9-iron with the same rhythm and tempo, finishing in balance. You don't need to hit balls to do this, just swing one of those clubs, then the other. It will work

Photo 11.1 "One-legged practice" keeps balance in tune.

wonders for your ability to maintain a consistent tempo on the golf course.

- When your game goes off, first check alignment. Set down practice clubs, address, look from your left eye alone, and make sure the ball, clubface, butt of the club, and your feet are in their correct relative positions. Have a partner check your shoulder alignment, as in the "buddy drill" (Photo 11.2).

Photo 11.2

- If your alignment seems fine, but your body motion feels sluggish or uncoordinated—particularly after a long layoff—have a partner perform bench drills with you (Photo 11.3), until you get a feeling of cohesive motion.

- Once the posture and alignment factors are in place, the ladder drill is your key to scoring. Practice it forever, every time you get a chance, on a rug or outdoors. You'll discover that there is a direct correlation between how much ladder practice you get and how well you score.

Photo 11.3

Self-Check:
It's Not How the Ball Is Flying—
It's How the Fundamentals Are Being Performed

Many fine players, including Bob Jones and Jack Nicklaus, said that they never felt they had matured until they could self-check and correct their games on the road.

I teach my players, at all levels, to be self-sufficient that way. It's important to me that they self-check, not in terms of how the ball is flying, but in terms of how they are performing their pre-swing skills. I don't want my student to arrive at the tournament or outing saying, "let me hit a few—well, the ball is slicing, so something is wrong."

I want players to be able to check their alignment, posture, hold of the club, and other factors in the hotel mirror without hitting balls, and be able to say something like, "I need work on my shoulder alignment, or I won't be playing well this weekend."

The more you practice the drills in this book, the more you develop a feel for when things are right, and when something is getting out of whack, before the ball is ever struck.

Drilling to master your pre-swing skills is the key to self-sufficiency.

Keeping a Good Attitude

This book is primarily about physical skills. But it's also invaluable to have a good mental attitude and approach.

Here is some of the specific advice I give students:

An Alert Attitude of Indifference

Play with "an alert attitude of indifference." I ran into this phrase in a golf instruction pamphlet by a fellow named Andy Petnuch, written many years ago, and I use it often with my students. They always seem to like it. It helps them relax. It means you're "all there," when you play, but you don't invest yourself too much in the result.

While I was working on this book, my daughter Kim talked to me about how my method of teaching was similar to that of Dr. Shinichi Suzuki, the Japanese professor of music. When I went down to Memphis and watched my granddaughter's violin class, I understood the similarity.

For teaching violin, Suzuki devised what he called "teaching points"—detailed instructional points covering the fundamentals of posture, the hold of the implement, etc, each "point" supported by drills to habituate. Often the drill did not involve holding the violin. And they were sequenced to produce an accumulation of skills.

This is very much how I teach. Just as Suzuki kept his students away from actually playing music, I keep my pupils away from actually playing golf shots, until they have absorbed good habits in detail. When I finally allow the student to play, the results are much better.

Don't Try to Predict the Future

Play golf in the present, not in the future. Don't forecast your shots, because not even the weatherman can do that. Golfers have a habit of thinking about various distracting things—a difficult hole coming up, whether they might birdie a certain par 5, and so on. Instead, play each shot the best you can, don't dwell in the past, don't anticipate the future.

Pre-Shot Routine, Post-Shot Routine

I recently gave a playing lesson to a scratch golfer who blew his stack during a round and quickly went from one-under to three-over. When we got to the clubhouse, I told him, "there's not only a pre-shot routine, there is a post-shot routine." Take pride in your poise after a bad shot. Make sure your next decision is a smart one. A little petulance is natural and allowable. But never allow anger and rash decision-making to snowball.

Ask Yourself, What is at Stake?

If pressure is getting to you on the golf course, or you're getting angry or upset, ask yourself how much, really, is at stake? Because in truth, *nothing* is at stake.

I served in the Army Signal Corps during the second World War, and I remember climbing up telegraph poles and cutting Nazi telegraph wires, or rehabilitating our own wires, while we were under fire. After that, what was really at stake on the golf course? Nothing.

And I know many of my students have been through situations of great danger, discomfort, or misery, or situations where they might lose their jobs, their families, or their lives. So what is at stake on the golf course? A little pride, maybe a few dollars, but really *nothing*.

That means, have fun, and don't get too wrapped up in how well you are performing. Above all, if you are having a bad day, don't get into an ill humor that affects the other members of your group. Stay positive.

Remember, you're very lucky to be on the course at all, because there are many worse places you might be.

Photo 11.4   When confronted with a narrow fairway "release your brakes" and swing freely.

Release Your Brakes

Some players have a tendency to tighten up on narrow driving holes—during playing lessons I will remind such a player, as he steps up onto the tee, "release your brakes." That has always been a good phrase for players—it relaxes them. Just let yourself go, and you'll do much better on average than if you tried to steer the ball down those fairways (Photo 11.4).

Keep Your Shoes On

I like to tell this to players who swing too hard. Some players start out at a pretty good swing pace but swing harder and harder as the round goes on. If you have that tendency, this is good advice to remember.

Good Player: Beware Perfectionism

Just as the slice is the bane of bad golfers, too much perfectionism is the bane of many good golfers. Perfectionism can take you a long way in improving your game—because you want to be stylish, you want to be "in the know" about what makes a better swing, you're willing to work—all these factors are helping you, but at a certain point, perfectionism starts to hurt, because you expect too much of yourself, and you expect things to always go well.

If you are a good player, realize that you are a human being, and you will make a lot of mistakes. There will be days when you will hit the ball badly. There will be distractions, there will be bad breaks. A gust of wind will ruin your shot, or you'll get a wrong yardage. These are tests of your equilibrium, and emotional equilibrium is worth much more than shotmaking perfection.

Tension, Pride, and Fear

Tension, pride and fear are destroyers of the golf swing. Most players are prone to one of them more than the other two. Figure out which one applies to you, and work on eliminating its influence.

When I began teaching, I dreamed that someday I would find a path to good golf so foolproof that I would be like the Pied Piper and lead the whole world to a better game. Since then I've realized what every pro does, that misinformation gets into the golfing population faster than good information can prevail against it.

There is always another generation coming along, slicing the ball, learning by trial and error, and asking, "what did I do there?" But at least I can have a positive effect on the games of my students, and, I hope, the readers of this book.

All I do in my lessons is give players "quiet hands" and good touch in the short game, get their ball position, body angles, and alignment perfect in the long game, and then watch them go. If they really follow my system, and do a lot of work without a golf club, they keep getting better and better.

A good example was Ms. Aleta Young, a student of mine at the Willow Glen course, near Chicago. When we were constructing my original website back in 2000, Aleta was asked to give a testimonial about my teaching. This was what she said:

"My husband of thirty years is a golfer, he plays very well, and kept wanting me to learn, and one day I weakened and said I should try the game. And he took me up on it, and got me five lessons from Julius.

"I had never met him, and I drove there thinking, what have I gotten myself into? And it was the best time I've had in ages. He was the ultimate teacher. He said, 'I have a system, and there are things you have to do before you hit a ball.' And I learned to enjoy the game, because I learned the correct things to do. It's amazing what you can do after only a couple of weeks of working with him.

"He finally let me hit a ball, and from the first time that I hit the ball, it went, 'whooosh!' And it kept on doing it, I hit it well right from the start."

Aleta was a teacher herself, and she instinctively understood the basis of my technique. She was also a disciplined worker, and she accepted the "delayed gratification" of not hitting balls until she was prepared.

The result was that she started out hitting the ball well and has done so ever since, advancing at the game without any major let-downs or disappointments.

I guarantee you, the rewards for sticking to your drilling, and progressing from short shots to long shots, are terrific.

In fact, we just contacted Aleta recently about how her game was going. She said she was playing very well indeed, was playing with her husband frequently now, and when they planned vacations, *she* was the one searching the brochures to make sure there would be a golf course nearby.

Because Aleta had the discipline to drill extensively without a golf club, she set herself up for a lifetime of enjoyment.

You can do the same.

Appendix 1
What I Hope to Give Young Teachers

This book is written primarily for the player who hopes to improve. But I believe it will also be helpful for the teacher. It's often the case with teaching pros that they originally dreamed of playing tournament golf, and teaching was "plan B."

For a young pro who has no teaching experience, the gap between his or her excellence and the student's mediocrity can seem too much to overcome. The pro muses, "I shoot 68. This person shoots 101. How can I even relate to him? He asks what he's doing wrong? He's doing everything wrong!"

Such a frustrated young pro, by working with this book, can learn to take things piece by piece. The journey in golf from mediocrity to excellence is an incremental one, and if the pro knows the progression of those increments, he or she can feel happy and satisfied simply getting the player to advance by one increment. There's no need to see the player go from 101 to 85 in one lesson. The pro only needs to see the player make that one incremental change, because the pro knows that eventually, with enough of these changes, the player will get to the 85, and even get to the 78, if the player has the determination.

That's where the teacher learns patience, not necessarily because he or she is patient by nature, but because there is a "road map" in mind, and there is faith in the eventual success of incremental change.

Another advantage to my system is that it's the sort of structure that other pros can build on and develop. They can work on their own "motion drills" to instill pre-swing skills. The particulars of my drills are always in the process of development. Even while this book was being written, for instance, I was changing my emphasis from the "grandfather clock" drill to the "bank the airplane" drill to teach spine tilt away from the target. The latter turned out to be more vivid, in giving students a feeling for this tilt.

The good habits never change, but the drills to instill them undergo a constant process of being perfected and added to. Young teaching pros can take this structure and work with it all their lives—taking it far beyond the point that I've taken it.

Appendix 2
"A Superb Teacher"
by Dr. Charles Henry,
Professor, African American Studies Department,
University of California—Berkeley

Why is a non-golfer writing this biographical essay about Julius Richardson? The simple answer is that this book is as much about the golf teacher as it is about golf. That is, the life experiences of Julius Richardson are an integral part of his approach to golf. This approach could not have been developed by someone in his or her thirties or forties. It took sixty-eight years for Julius Richardson to begin teaching it seriously and another twelve to perfect it.

Someone who was only a student of the game could not have developed the Richardson approach to golf. Julius is first and foremost a student of people. He likes people, is curious about them, and wants to help them. Born a coal-miner's son in Greensburg, Pennsylvania in 1921, Julius's father, John, was a great role model. He was a hard-working, family man that expected the most out of his sons, Julius and Albert. There were always neighbors and boarders in the house as Julius's mother, Marie, took care of them all cooking, sewing, playing the piano and singing.

These positive influences did not mean that Julius always followed the straight and narrow path. He was always adventurous and always questioning. He wanted to see the big cities and larger world and at age thirteen caught freight trains and traveled around the Mid-West. His nature led him to leave high school and join the

famous 10th Calvary unit of the U. S. Army in 1940. Despite the disappointment to his parents in the long run his military experience would prove very beneficial.

Julius landed at Omaha Beach shortly after D-Day and was in the Battle of the Bulge. He married for the first time and had two children while in the service. After the War a serious car accident shocked him into finishing high school and planning his future.

Just as he was beginning to get his life together he was called back into the service for the Korean War. He participated in the underwater tests of the hydrogen bomb in the Marshall Islands. He also started going to night school where he met his second wife, Margaret. It was around then that a Pittsburgh buddy took him golfing and teased him about his lack of skill on the golf course.

Julius responded to the challenge by taking golfing lessons. As

luck would have it, Richard Grout, the brother of Jack Grout who trained Jack Nicklaus, was one of the instructors at Scott Air Force Base where Julius was stationed at this time. That was the turning point for Julius. Within two years he was able to beat his Pittsburgh buddy. However, an accident forced him to quit the game for five years.

After 20 years of military service, Julius got a civilian position as an inspector and later a light measurement technician in meteorology at the Newark, Ohio Air Force Aerospace Station. It was the 1960s and Julius became involved in a host of civic activities including the Boy Scouts, United Way, Mental Health, Council of Churches, Celebrity Speaker's Club and the A.M.E. church. It was through his role as a Sunday school teacher that I came to know Julius and his family, which had grown to include four daughters-Julieanne, Sabrina, Gail and Kim. Julius became my "honorary godfather" as he took an interest in the development of me and several other young boys.

We listened to him because his approach was not to say, "Do this but don't do that." Instead, he would sit down with us and carefully have us go over the possible consequences of any action we might be thinking from buying a car to choosing a college. These sessions would often last until the wee hours of the morning.

It was in Newark that Julius took up the game of golf again. However, both his civic and personal commitments as well as his work in promoting equal employment opportunity at the Aerospace Station, prevented him from playing as much golf as he wanted. Retiring from the Aerospace Station he moved to Columbus, Ohio and began selling insurance full-time. Due to his extraordinary ability to relate to people, Julius quickly rose to the elite million-dollar club in insurance sales.

After putting all of his daughters through college, which he regards as his greatest accomplishment, Julius moved to Chicago to help daughter Julieanne start a business. With more free time on his hands he began to play seriously at Naval Station Great Lakes. He was so successful that within a short time he was asked to become the pro there. Julius then began to travel south to teach and eventually began working with the Ben Hogan Tour. After five years of teaching he joined the United States Golf Teachers Federation and

became credentialed. When *Golf Magazine* voted him one of the top 100 golf teachers and the United States Golf Teachers Federation named him the "Teacher of the Century," it was a fitting tribute to a life that placed people, not golf, first.

Perhaps in another era Julius would have been a great tour player. We could have all enjoyed watching him but we would not have the benefit of his accumulated wisdom. As you will see, he tells you what you already know—that you need to be physically fit and practice. And then he tells you something you don't know-that you will be your own best teacher. You will need to remember that in the days and years ahead because as Julius says, "You can love golf but it won't love you back!"

Appendix 3
Skill Building Drills:
Alphabetical and by Concept

Alphabetical Listing

Concept Listing

Index

What people are saying about

Better Golf
A Skill Building Approach

"I think Julius is a breath of fresh air in the world of golf instruction. Julius' teaching is based on building control, starting with the short shots and going foreword from there. He helps students prepare . . . with a little training of this kind, players can shoot lower scores and have a lot more fun playing the game."
—From the *Foreword* by Bob Toski,
World Golf Teachers Hall of Fame

"Julius Richardson is not afraid to teach the game in his own unique style. It is a systematic process that other golf professionals would benefit from adopting. If you follow Richardson's skill building formula, you'll be well on your way to lower scores."
—Lorin Anderson,
Managing Editor, *Golf Magazine*

"To watch Julius in action is to watch a well choreographed professional at work. His eye and uncanny understanding of the golf swing, and willingness to still keep learning truly have him in an elevated league of his own."
—Geoff Bryant, President,
United States Golf Teachers Federation

"My good friend, and golf's great friend, Julius Richardson, has a brilliant and simple approach to teaching—solid fundamentals allow the mind to focus exclusively on the target—and target orientation leads to lower scores and maximum joy. Freedom of action is hidden behind your long checklist of do's and don'ts."
—Peter Kessler, Broadcaster
and Senior Writer, *Golf Magazine*

For additional copies of

Better Golf: A Skill Building Approach

Order from: Warde Publishers, Inc.
530 University Avenue, Suite 102-7
Palo Alto, CA 94301
Toll-free order line: (800) 699-2733

ORDER FORM

Please send _____ copy(ies) of *Better Golf: A Skill Building Approach* by Julius Richardson and Mark Gearen at $29.95. (Please add $4.50 for first copy and $.50 for each additional copy for packing and shipping. California residents, add $2.47 sales tax per book ordered.) Make check payable to Warde Publishers, Inc.   Total enclosed: $_____

Name _____

Organization _____

Address _____

City _____ State _____ Zip _____

Phone _____